Cambridge Elements

Elements in Historical Theory and Practice
edited by
Daniel Woolf
Queen's University, Ontario

GENDER, THEORY, AND HISTORY

On the Knowledge and Politics of Bodies

María Inés La Greca
*National University of Tres de Febrero,
National Scientific and Technical Research Council, and
University of Buenos Aires*

Shaftesbury Road, Cambridge CB2 8EA, United Kingdom

One Liberty Plaza, 20th Floor, New York, NY 10006, USA

477 Williamstown Road, Port Melbourne, VIC 3207, Australia

314–321, 3rd Floor, Plot 3, Splendor Forum, Jasola District Centre, New Delhi – 110025, India

103 Penang Road, #05–06/07, Visioncrest Commercial, Singapore 238467

Cambridge University Press is part of Cambridge University Press & Assessment, a department of the University of Cambridge.

We share the University's mission to contribute to society through the pursuit of education, learning and research at the highest international levels of excellence.

www.cambridge.org
Information on this title: www.cambridge.org/9781009571845

DOI: 10.1017/9781009372459

© María Inés La Greca 2025

This publication is in copyright. Subject to statutory exception and to the provisions of relevant collective licensing agreements, no reproduction of any part may take place without the written permission of Cambridge University Press & Assessment.

When citing this work, please include a reference to the DOI 10.1017/9781009372459

First published 2025

A catalogue record for this publication is available from the British Library

ISBN 978-1-009-57184-5 Hardback
ISBN 978-1-009-37241-1 Paperback
ISSN 2634-8616 (online)
ISSN 2634-8608 (print)

Cambridge University Press & Assessment has no responsibility for the persistence or accuracy of URLs for external or third-party internet websites referred to in this publication and does not guarantee that any content on such websites is, or will remain, accurate or appropriate.

For EU product safety concerns, contact us at Calle de José Abascal, 56, 1°, 28003 Madrid, Spain, or email eugpsr@cambridge.org

Gender, Theory, and History

On the Knowledge and Politics of Bodies

Elements in Historical Theory and Practice

DOI: 10.1017/9781009372459
First published online: November 2025

María Inés La Greca
*National University of Tres de Febrero,
National Scientific and Technical Research Council, and
University of Buenos Aires*

Author for correspondence: María Inés La Greca, mlagreca@untref.edu.ar

Abstract: The category of gender has a special relation to history as an academic practice, as a form of writing, and as a way of understanding humanity as such. This Element reconstructs the trajectory of debates over gender to trace its emergence as an analytical category through the work of feminist thinkers such as that by Joan W. Scott, Judith Butler, and Donna Haraway. Situating the reader in a twenty-first-century perspective, this Element shows that gender is still a key term in theoretical discussions not only within but also beyond academia, in current public debates related to women and LGBTQ+ human rights around the globe. "Gender" is both a theoretical resource and a political tool to effect social change. Refiguring gender as a historical category, this Element provides a promising framework for historians, theorists of history, and everyone interested in reflecting on the relation between bodies, knowledge, and politics.

Keywords: gender, feminist theory, theory of history, Joan W. Scott, Judith Butler, Donna Haraway

© María Inés La Greca 2025

ISBNs: 9781009571845 (HB), 9781009372411 (PB), 9781009372459 (OC)
ISSNs: 2634-8616 (online), 2634-8608 (print)

Contents

1 Introduction: Why Gender Still Matters?   1

2 The Emergence of Gender as an Analytical Category   6

3 The Historicity of Gender: Knowledge, Power, and Bodies   20

4 Gender, Past and Present of the Theory of History: A Relational View of Embodiment   59

References   65

1 Introduction: Why Gender Still Matters?

The category of gender is an undeniable contribution of feminist theory to several disciplinary fields. Although gender is an interdisciplinary category from the start, it has a special relation to history as an academic practice, as a form of writing, and as a way of understanding humanity as such. The challenge of giving an account of the relationship between history and gender from a theoretical point of view is a fascinating and complex one, given the different philosophical, linguistic, epistemic, and political aspects this reflection entails. Theorizing gender requires that we reconsider how history has been written, who has been part of historical narratives and who has been left out, and who is the subject of historical writing both as the agent and the theme of historical reflection. Thus, an approach to gender from the perspective of contemporary theory of history should not focus solely on gender history in terms of the research done in relation to it as an object of historical study. It should aim at a deeper level of reflection to underscore how the concept of gender *is historical*: it is in itself a historical emergent, both as an analytical category and as a way of interpreting individual and social identity.

Moreover, gender is still a key term in theoretical discussions within humanities, social, and natural sciences and beyond academia, in public debates related to women and LGBTIQ+ human rights around the globe. What we understand by "gender" affects the way that research is carried forward in several disciplines as much as it contributes to arguments presented in national and international institutions and organizations in charge of the promotion of sex-gender policies. Thus, gender, history, theory, and politics are intimately related insofar as our comprehension of "what sex and gender are" is deeply rooted in basic cultural assumptions of what "human beings" are. As Judith Butler puts it, gender figures as a precondition for the production and maintenance of human legibility (2004, 11).

However, basic cultural assumptions can be challenged both from developments in scientific research and critical thinking and from social movements when subaltern or marginalized subjects raise their voice against the inequalities and violence that those assumptions entail for them. Regarding sex-gender issues, this has been the case: gender is a category developed within feminist theory both as a critical resource to rethink scientific bodies of knowledge and as a political resource to effect change in society at large. Nevertheless, this relationship between knowledge and power, science and politics, is not an easy one to grasp.

Structure of This Element

An overview of the emergence of the category of gender in its historical context and the debates that surrounded it presents an excellent opportunity for a current and updated reflection on the relations between sex, gender, history, and theoretical and political change. To that aim, in Sections 2 and 3, I will present a theoretically informed reconstruction of the chronology of the development of gender as a category for historical analysis. My emplotment will put forward a story of the emergence, establishment, and critical reworkings of gender in feminist and historical theory. In Section 2, I will map the original proposals of gender as an analytical category in the late seventies and eighties in US academia and how it gained scientific status and global impact in the eighties with the consolidation of gender studies as a disciplinary (and interdisciplinary) field. I will take Joan Wallach Scott's seminal work in the theorization of the notion of gender as my main point of focus because it constitutes a thorough and critical review of the first decade of research in historical studies. Scott's work also functions as a consolidation and refinement of gender as an analytical category and at the same time it became a turning point in the field given the impact of the linguistic turn, or more specifically, poststructuralism.[1] However, I will also show that by the end of the eighties the category of gender was challenged regarding its explanatory limits and assumptions. This also included explicit self-criticism from the feminist theorists who champion it originally, most notably, Scott. This section will arrive at what seems to be a tragic narrative of the "rise and fall" of the category of gender.

In Section 3, I will present the severe criticism gender underwent within feminist theory debates since the late eighties and nineties that explains the seemingly tragic narrative presented in the previous section. The reflection on this criticism has two aims: first, to underscore the critical gains that feminist theory achieved through these debates around gender, and second, to offer an alternative interpretation of this theoretical process. Instead of the "fall" of gender's usefulness as a category of analysis, I will claim that it underwent a refiguration as a *historical* category. Hence, I propose to abandon the tragic narrative and replace it with a different retrospective take from the vantage point of the present context, where the meaning of gender is, again, openly contested. I will elaborate here on the fundamental contribution of the theory of gender performativity by Judith Butler and how it amounted to a revision of the binary and heterosexist assumptions left unquestioned in the original definition of

---

[1] In this Element I will refer to Scott's (and later, Butler's) position as "poststructuralist," and not "postmodernist." For an argument on the differences between these labels and the preference for "poststructuralism" to classify their work, see Butler and Scott (1992).

gender as social construction and different from "sex" as the given, "natural" form of human bodies. The critical work of black feminist thinkers and the emergence of intersectional studies will also be necessary to understand the need to revise the race blind spots in some analyses of the sex-gender system. Also, Donna Haraway's reflection on situated knowledges will be key to grasp the relationship between knowledge and power, bodies and meanings. These reflections also contributed to elaborating a nuanced understanding of the idea of gender as a social construction.

Section 3 will end with a general map of new academic fields that since the nineties intersected polemically with sex-gender research or that contributed to its critical reconsideration, such as queer theory and trans studies, posthumanism and new materialism, decolonial, and antiracist research. Although it is not possible to give an exhaustive overview of these more recent developments, I will highlight how they offer lines of research indebted to Butler's and Haraway's theories while they also take a critical stance toward them. Finally, the work on gender, race, and epistemic injustice by José Medina will allow me to reconnect the theoretical reconstruction of the concept of gender with its epistemic and political relevance in current public debates related to women and LGBTIQ+ human rights around the globe.

In Section 4, this Element will claim that the trajectory of feminist debates that leads us to a refigured notion of gender as a historical category also offers a promising take on the relation between bodies, knowledge, and politics that we can define as *a relational view of embodiment*. This view retains the critical insight of gender as a social construction in a sophisticated way, but at the same time it rejects biological determinism. Moreover, the implications of this view for historical writing offer an opportunity to reread a certain narrative on the past and present of the theory of history and to link its concerns to current public debates. In sum, this Element aims at providing historians and theorists of history critical resources to incorporate in their practice a more complex understanding of embodiment and its relations to categories of identity.

Before we dive into the "origins" of the category of gender, it is key for this Element to acknowledge its own context of emergence, situating the reader in a twenty-first-century perspective. Thus, this Element will show that gender is still a key term inside and outside academia, given the current context of global debates in the public sphere where gender is the object of dispute between its advocates and its detractors in relation to human rights legislation and to national and international policy regarding women and LGBTIQ+ people.

Context

We are currently witnessing a lively momentum of social movements: feminist, LGBTIQ+, queer, and trans activist groups that take the streets in different parts of the globe to claim their place in a broader, more complex, and democratic notion of humanity and, hence, equal rights, political recognition, and better living situations. A common demand of these movements is that *gender* violence and *femi*cide must stop. That was the central claim of the *Ni Una Menos* ("not one less") protests in Argentina that, since 2015, have provoked a massive social movement. These protests were echoed throughout Latin America and the globe. Moreover, transnational ties between activists have evolved and extended across countries and continents, with the organization of the International Women's Strike every March 8th since 2017. This process has been testified by the publication of new manifestos such as *Feminist for the 99%, A Manifesto* by Arruza, Bhattacharya, and Fraser (2019), and *Feminist International. How to Change Everything* by Gago (2020). Even social media has been the realm of strong debates and integral to political articulations such as those around the hashtags #Niunamenos or the so-called #MeToo movement. "Gender talk," in this sense, is everywhere.

However, this explicit protagonism of "gender" is not only related to the use done by those who strive for justice and equality for people who have been marginalized or subjected to violence. Gender also appears in public debates due to a global movement that presents itself as *anti-gender*, as opposing a "gender ideology." This counter-movement has come to be known globally as a "conservative backlash" against feminist and LGBTIQ+ struggles (Butler 2019).

In *Who Is Afraid of Gender?* (2024) Butler shows that the issue of gender has been a central one in presidential elections in Brazil, Costa Rica, Colombia, France, Switzerland, the United Kingdom, Scotland, Ecuador, and Germany (43). This is due not solely to the demands of social movements that strive for sex-gender justice, but it is also related to the influence that those supporting the anti-gender movement have had in government decisions (or attempts) to abolish gender studies programs in the universities or Sex Education in primary and secondary school (e.g., in the United States and Hungary). In this case, "anti-gender talk" has been part of political declarations or party proposals in Spain, Italy, and Russia.

We found, then, two opposite attitudes toward gender today as witnessed by, on the one hand, a reemergence of political demands from the feminist and LGBTIQ+ movement against gender violence on a global scale; and, on the other hand, the rise of the backlash against "gender ideology" that opposes

Human Rights legislation such as protection for women against gender violence, same-sex marriage, trans people access to gender-affirming health care, and so on. To the extent that the advancement in political freedom challenges very basic cultural assumptions, there are social groups that react against the change on the status quo. Although the accusation that gender relates to a destructive ideology is untenable (as shown in Butler 2019 and 2024), definitions of sex, gender, and sexuality reveal a close relationship between knowledge and politics.

The reader may, then, ask: how does the trajectory of debates over gender that this Element traces relate to this contemporary context?

Let me give you a hint by presenting a key moment of the story *in media res*: in 1999, Joan W. Scott published a revised edition of her 1988 book *Gender and the Politics of History*. On the cover, it says: "The classic work, now with a preface and a new chapter reassessing the usefulness of the gender category." In the new preface, Scott relates the controversy over the use of "gender" at the United Nations Fourth World Conference on Women held in Beijing in 1995. Some Republican congressmen and delegates from right-to-life groups criticized the use of the term as implying per se an attack on morality and family values and blamed the gender feminists participating in the UN program for this, given that they "believe that everything we think as natural, including motherhood and fatherhood, heterosexuality, marriage, and the family, are only culturally 'fixes' originated by men to oppress women. These feminists profess that such roles have been socially constructed and are therefore subject to change" (ix). The controversy was of such proportions that there was a resolution added as an appendix to the Program of Action of the conference titled "Statement on the Commonly Understood Meaning of the Term 'Gender'." As Scott explains, nothing really informative came out of that statement: it claimed that the word was being used "in ordinary, generally accepted usage" in other UN conferences without "any new meaning or connotation" (x). What was interesting for Scott was that the definition of such "generally accepted usage" was nowhere to be found, as if the meaning were self-evident. In sum, to settle the controversy, the statement denied that it existed. Scott, then, claims:

> There is no question that serious differences were being debated in the furor over "gender", but, oddly, the term itself was beside the point. In ordinary usage, "gender" had become a synonym for the differences between sexes, both ascribed and "natural". Although it still could provoke heated debate and widespread anxiety among feminists as well as their critics, "gender" no longer transformed or destabilized political discourse, although it did give

proponents of women's equality a way of arguing that social roles were "socially constructed" and, therefore, open to change (x–xi).

Scott then recounts the important theoretical work that "gender" did in the feminist theory of the seventies and eighties, its usefulness and destabilizing effect, and how it also "seemed the best way to realize the goal of historians of women in the seventies: to bring women from the margins to the center of historical focus and, in the process, transform the way all history was written" (xi). But in 1999, Scott believes that "gender" has lost its critical edge, its radical academic and political agency (xii).

Although Scott is considered one of the feminist thinkers who championed the term "gender" in the eighties (Meyerowitz 2008; Smith 2013), at the end of the nineties, she claimed to be using the term less and less in her work given that she considered its critical potential to be exhausted. Nevertheless, in the paragraph quoted, Scott recognized that some of its political potential remained insofar as it still gave proponents of women's equality a way of arguing that social roles were "socially constructed" and, therefore, open to change. Here is the answer to the question I recently posed: by reviewing the narrative on the "rise and fall" of the category of gender that appeared in the nineties, we will trace how the insight that it is a "social construction" has been refigured in light of theoretical and political debates. Since the category of gender is both a theoretical achievement in feminist theory and a political resource to defend women and LGBTIQ+ rights, this Element provides the reader with valuable knowledge to explore the intimate relationship between knowledge, politics, and bodies.

2 The Emergence of Gender as an Analytical Category

"Origins" of the Category of Gender in Feminist Theory

"Gender" became a key analytical category for feminist theory during the 1970s. A general definition of gender would state that it is "a way of referring to the social organization of the relationship between the sexes" (Scott 1999, 28). With this term, feminists "wanted to insist on the fundamentally social quality of distinctions based on sex" (29). At its core, the use of the term "gender" meant a theoretically and politically justified rejection of biological determinism: differences between women and men in relation to their access to resources, power, and opportunities were not grounded in their biological endowment or "nature" but in specific (unequal) social arrangements.

Through the eighties, gender studies blossomed as a new interdisciplinary field of research. The analytical category of gender was elaborated as a more promising way of inquiring about women's oppression than those that focused solely on the notion of "women" and/or women's experiences as a separate object of study. As Bonnie Smith explains:

> The idea behind gender is that it is not enough to study women as a unique group to come to a true and useful understanding of women's situation – including their past and present condition. Rather, one needs to take into account men's lives as well: the entire male-female organization of society, a family, or a workplace contains essential information. One cannot simply investigate women to understand violence, economic inequity, or the place of women in political processes; the field of gender relations holds the key to the situation of women (...) Most matters pertaining to women's identities unfold in some form of male-female relationship, including the overall values of society when it comes to masculinity and femininity. For some, that relationship may constitute an important duality that is a basic building block of the world (2013, 82).

Gender refers to a relational understanding of masculinity and femininity. Hence, it is not a synonym for "women," although some public and lay uses of the term tend to presuppose that it is. Here we must first clarify that gender is a technical or specific category within feminist theory, but it is also a notion that pervades nonacademic discourses. It has a life of its own that exceeds its theoretical use, as we saw in the previous paragraph. The fascinating fact about the concept of gender is how it travels through different contexts and how it functions similarly and differently in them at the same time. In Smith's words, "Beyond the assertion of gender's relevance, however, definitions of the term are highly variable" (83). Moreover, the borders of those different contexts may be porous and "contaminate" the uses of the term in relevant ways. Donna Haraway also stressed this issue: "The value of an analytical category is not necessarily annulled by critical consciousness of its historical specificity and cultural limits. But feminist concepts of gender raise sharply the problems of cultural comparison, linguistic translation, and political solidarity" (1991, 130).

Although one task of this Element is to offer a definition of gender, we would lose much of the complexity of the term and its uses if the definition does not acknowledge that variability. In fact, what should be offered are *definitions* of gender. Hence, this Element analyzes the emergence of the category of gender within US feminist theory, but to claim that the term has its "origins" there is another issue.

From the present vantage point, we can trace a conventional narration of that origin and its critical revision: there is a general assumption that feminist theorists coined the term gender to study the unequal and hierarchical relations between women and men in sexist societies, exporting the notion from its original grammatical use (Scott 1999, xi subscribed this narrative). However, this common narrative is not accurate since the notion of gender and its fundamental distinction from "sex," was exported by US feminist theorists from its use during the fifties and sixties in the research done in medicine by John Money (in relation to what then was called "hermaphroditism" and today we call intersexuality) and in psychiatry by Robert Stoller (in relation to gender identity in transsexual people).[2] As Sara Ahmed claims, "We know that feminists have disagreed about how to understand sex and gender as social categories; we inherit them, we did not invent them. We know that part of the work of feminism is to contest that inheritance" (2021, 3; see also Haraway 1991, 132–135).

Another undeniable influence in feminist definitions of gender was Simone de Beauvoir's *The Second Sex* (1952), although she did not use the term "gender."[3] After studying the claims on the nature and reality of women from the biology, psychoanalysis, and historical materialism of her time, Beauvoir concluded that one is not born but rather becomes (or is made) a woman:

> From then in, there was a steady intellectual movement toward uncovering the artificial nature of all gender distinctions. That is, the interrelated behaviors of men and women – or "gender" – were not natural; they were cultural and constructed by human society and human beliefs.
> Thus, Simone de Beauvoir's *Second Sex* was a crucial moment in advancing more relational ideas about gender as a fabrication (Smith 2013, 85–86).[4]

Beauvoir's philosophical contribution and the force of the women's movement of the sixties and seventies inspired US feminist thinkers to use the concept of gender to give theoretical form to two basic claims: that biology is not destiny and that the personal is political. Women's oppression and the distribution of power, resources, and rights that privileged men were not the result of a fixed or deterministic "nature" or "biology." Women's lives were not

---

[2] It must be said that Stoller's and Money's research has been criticized both by the intersex and trans communities for contributing to pathologizing their identities. Haraway claimed that "'Second-wave' feminist politics around 'biological determinism' vs. 'social constructionism' and the biopolitics of sex/gender differences occur within discursive fields pre-structured by the gender identity paradigm crystallized in the 1950s and 60s. The gender identity paradigm was a functionalist and essentializing version of Simone de Beauvoir's 1940s insight that one is not born a woman" (1991, 133). More recently, Butler explained that although "gender" as a term was brought by Money to contemporary parlance, "that hardly means that gender theory and gender studies follow from Money's framework" (2024, 195). For a thorough discussion on Money's influence in gender studies and the specific feminist reworking of "gender," see Germon (2009).

[3] Published originally in France in 1949 as *Le Deuxième Sexe* by Libraire Gallimard.

[4] Smith also considers the work by anthropologists like Margaret Mead in the thirties and forties as key contributions to the idea that differences between men and women were constructed or artificial (2013, 85).

condemned to a "destiny" of subordination. The unequal relation between men and women could end by collective, political transformation.

This meant that women saw themselves as political agents and that they realized that their "personal" pain, disadvantages, or the violence suffered was not an individual anecdote but related to power arrangements and, hence, subject to change.[5] If the hierarchical understanding of the notions of femininity and masculinity was historical and political, then it was contingent, not necessary: in other words, "not rooted" in physical referents as the supposed "natural" anatomical difference of male and female.

A pioneer conceptualization and founding text of gender studies undoubtedly is "The Traffic in Women. Notes on the 'Political Economy' of Sex" published by anthropologist Gayle Rubin in 1975.[6] Situating her inquiry in the Marxist tradition, Rubin offers the notion "sex/gender system" to study what are "the relationships by which a female becomes an oppressed woman" (2011, 34). Rubin initially defines it as "the set of arrangements by which a society transforms biological sexuality into products of human activity, and in which these transformed sexual needs are satisfied" (2011, 34). As she explains:

> We usually call the system by which elements of the natural world are transformed into objects of human consumption the "economy." But the needs that are satisfied by economic activity even in the richest, Marxian sense do not exhaust fundamental human requirements. A human group must also reproduce itself from generation to generation. The needs of sexuality and procreation must be satisfied as much as the need to eat, and one of the most obvious deductions to be made from the data of anthropology is that these needs are hardly ever satisfied in any "natural" form, any more that are the needs for food. Hunger is hunger, but what counts as food is culturally determined and obtained. Every society has some form of organized economic activity. Sex is sex, but what counts as sex is equally culturally determined and obtained (39).

Rubin then claims that every society also has a "sex/gender system" that she defines as "a set of arrangements by which the biological raw material of human sex and procreation is shaped by human, social intervention and satisfied in a conventional manner, no matter how bizarre some of those conventions may be." Rubin argues that sex-gender system is a better categorial lens to study women's oppression than the notion of patriarchy and the Marxist notion of mode of reproduction. The three notions coincide in their attempt to distinguish sexual systems from economic ones and give them proper, autonomous

---
[5] For a reflection on the relationship between women's agency, writing, and feminist history, see La Greca (2023).
[6] From here on, I will quote the version of this article published in Rubin (2011).

consideration (i.e., not reducing sexual oppression to the economic mode of production). However, Rubin believes that "sex/gender system" is more useful since it contributes to another key distinction:

> between the human capacity and necessity to create a sexual world, and the empirically oppressive ways in which sexual worlds have been organized. *Patriarchy* subsumes both meanings into the same term. *Sex/gender system*, on the other hand, is a neutral term that refers to the domain and indicates that oppression is not inevitable in that domain but is the product of the specific social relations which organize it (40).

Rubin theorized this notion by engaging critically with three theories: the failed attempt by Marx and Engels to think the oppression of women in their writings; Lévi-Strauss's structuralist approach to kinship and the exchange of women; and Freud's and Lacan's psychoanalysis as a theory of sexuality. Although Rubin's groundbreaking article deserves a more extensive presentation, I will only comment briefly on her feminist use of these previous theories to communicate the originality of her work.

From Lévi-Strauss, Rubin takes the explanation of how the passage to culture was produced by securing social relationships through the exchange of gifts: not only things but also women. Given that the incest taboo "imposes the social aim of exogamy and alliance upon the biological events of sex and procreation" (44), women are exchanged in matrimony to secure relationships between men, producing not only reciprocity but also kinship. Rubin sees here, however, another underlying taboo: that on homosexuality since exogamy is understood heterosexually. Rubin, hence, finds in Lévi-Strauss a theory of kinship that maps at the same time the oppression of women since they can only be objects, but not subjects of exchange. Also, the notion of the exchange of women places the oppression of women within social systems and not in biology. As Rubin will point out about psychoanalysis, too, the theory describes the oppression of women but does not recognize it or name it as such.

In relation to psychoanalysis, Rubin considers it a feminist theory *manqué* insofar as it contains a theory of human sexuality and "a description of the mechanism by which the sexes are divided and deformed, of how bisexual, androgynous infants are transformed into boys and girls" (48) through the Oedipus complex and fear of castration. Freud and Lacan offer "a description of how phallic culture domesticates women, and the effects for women of their domestication" (56). Rubin credits Lacan's reading of Freud for further removing from psychoanalytic theory on gender identity its features of biological determinism. However, again, psychoanalysis traces this process but does not denounce its oppressive effects on women.

Among Rubin's conclusions, she stressed that the sex/gender system was not immutably oppressive and that it should be reorganized through political action (60–61): "we are not only oppressed *as* women; we are oppressed by having to *be* women – or men as the case may be" (61). Hence, Rubin claimed that the feminist movement should not only eliminate the oppression of women but also obligatory sexualities and sex roles to create a society where "one's sexual anatomy is irrelevant to who one is, what one does, and with whom one makes love" (2011, 34). Key gender theorists such as Joan W. Scott and Judith Butler will provide their reflections on gender as critical developments of Rubin's ideas.

Through this very brief presentation, we arrive at a first sense in which studying gender relates to theory and history and to the intimate relation between the knowledge and politics of bodies. The use of gender as a category of analysis implied several claims about the relationship between male and female bodies that were critical of previous ways of understanding it:

1. That the hierarchical and unequal relationship between men and women was not a natural fact, but artificial: a construction.
2. That this construction was of a historical, cultural kind. It was the result of a history of society, of arrangements that were taken for granted in a culture's given moment.
3. That this construction could be rejected and transformed.
4. That even if anatomical or biological differences were considered natural and unchangeable, historical arrangements were not.
5. Hence, the assumption of an opposition between nature and culture was key to understand the difference between "sex" and "gender."

The political potential of this distinction was that it allowed the denouncement of current women's oppression as a historical reality that needed not be so. These claims were integral to the understanding, during the eighties, of gender as a *social construction*.

There is a theory of history implied in considering gender, men's and women's psychic formations, and social arrangements as "constructed" rather than "natural." History is culture, and it is the other of nature. Also, historicity becomes the name of what is not necessary and, hence, subject to social and political transformation. At the same time, biology as nature is reduced to fixity, necessity, and what is "given." If "sex" names the natural features of embodiment, then there remains something that is unchangeable by human will or culture. But this is not a problematic claim (yet) since disentangling and releasing gender from sex was the central theoretical and political move to claim that present unequal relations between men and women were not justified in their different biological constitution or endowment. It was not biology that was rejected, but the assumption that it was a natural difference that explained and justified social and political ones.

Joan W. Scott's Theorization of Gender

Joan Wallach Scott's seminal work "Gender: A Useful Category of Historical Analysis," published in 1986, marks the consolidation of the category of gender (along with the emerging field of gender studies) during the eighties.[7] Scott's piece was a thorough and critical review of the first decade of research guided by the notion of gender in historical studies, from the seventies to the first half of the eighties. Building critically from previous approaches, Scott offers a theory of gender through the refinement of the notion as an analytical category. As Meyerowitz (2008) has claimed, Scott championed the theorization of gender for historical studies in what remains one of the more cited papers in the discipline. Even today, Scott's text is considered a must-read for anyone interested in understanding what gender is. In other words, it is a classic.

This article was also a critical intervention in the theory of history of that time, a paradigmatic testimony of the impact of Foucault's and Derrida's work in historical studies and feminist history, which was labeled as a linguistic or poststructuralist turn. Moreover, Scott's original theorization inaugurated at the same time a critical turning point in gender studies: by fully introducing a poststructuralist perspective on history, discourse, and identity, Scott's piece paved the way for the growing distrust over the "usefulness" of the category her own work became synonym with. Poststructuralist feminist inquiries, such as Scott's, will lead at the end of the eighties and beginning of the nineties to a profound criticism of the founding distinction of the category: that between sex as biologically given and gender as historical or cultural, particularly in the work of Judith Butler.

To understand Scott's theorization in this double role of consolidation and turning point, let us start by analyzing its original formulation. Scott presents her definition of gender, claiming that it has two parts and several subsets that, although they are interrelated, must be analytically distinct. She continues:

> The core of the definition rests on an integral connection between two propositions: gender is a constitutive element of social relationships based on perceived differences between the sexes, and gender is a primary way of signifying relationships of power. Changes in the organization of social

---

[7] The article was first published in the *American Historical Review* 91 (5) in December 1986. From here on, I will quote the version published in Scott (1999).

relationships always correspond to changes in representations of power, but the direction of change is not necessarily one way (Scott 1999, 42–43).

The integral connection between the first and the second part of the definition becomes clearer when Scott explains that the theorizing of gender is developed in the second proposition. When Scott presents the four subsets or interrelated elements that make up the first part, she incorporates the different aspects of social relationships "based on perceived differences between the sexes" that should be considered to trace its workings as gendered relationships. These aspects have been identified through Scott's review of the previous decade of scholarship on gender. Her own definition builds on previous research and incorporates the different forms in which gender appears in history and social life. At the same time, Scott offers a theorization of gender that aims to overcome the limits or shortcomings of those precedent studies.

The first part of the definition, then, involves: (1) "culturally available symbols that evoke multiple (and often contradictory) representations" (43) – Scott gives the example of Eve and Mary as symbols of woman in the Western Christian tradition; (2) "normative concepts that set forth interpretations of the meanings of the symbols, that attempt to limit and contain their metaphoric possibilities." She adds that these concepts are expressed in religious, educational, scientific, legal, and political doctrines "and typically take the form of a fixed binary opposition, categorically and unequivocally asserting the meaning of male and female, masculine and feminine" (43); (3) a notion of politics and reference to social institutions and organization; and (4) subjective identity.

When introducing each subset, Scott explains the way they interrelate with each other. In the case of (1) culturally available symbols and (2) normative concepts of gender, the historian should inquire "Which symbolic representations are invoked, how and in what contexts" but this question must bear in mind that the multiple and often contradictory meanings those symbols evoke were being limited and contained by normative concepts:

> In fact, these normative statements depend on the refusal or repression of alternative possibilities, and sometimes overt contests about them take place (at what moments and under what circumstances ought to be a concern for historians). The position that emerges as dominant, however, is stated as the only possible one. Subsequent history is written as if these normative positions were the product of social consensus rather than conflict (43).

As we see, Scott is thinking through historical research with a Foucauldian–Derridean frame of mind: "The point of new historical investigation is to disrupt the notion of fixity, to discover the nature of the debate or repression that leads to the appearance of timeless permanence in binary gender representation." (43).

For the third element, Scott clearly wants to have a broader notion than those found in previous research that, for example, restricted gender to the kinship system. Thus, she includes here kinship along with the labor market, education, and the polity without reducing these aspects to one (especially kinship, since here Scott's reference is the work of Rubin). It is through all these aspects of social life that gender is constructed, for Scott: for example, in terms of sex-segregated labor, single-sex or coeducational institutions, or access to suffrage. Scott stresses that all four elements of the first proposition should be considered and that no one of them operates without the others. Yet they do not operate simultaneously, with one simply reflecting the others: "A question for historical research is, in fact, what the relationships among the four aspects are." (44).

This is clear also in the way that the fourth element relates to the previous ones, while being analytically distinct. The fourth aspect is gender as subjective identity and here Scott acknowledges the contribution of feminist theorizations of gender that build from psychoanalysis, specifically, Lacanian theory and Rubin's work.

In the presentation of the third element, Scott considers Rubin's view insofar as it related contemporary gender issues to "older kinship systems based on the exchange of women" (44) instead of paying attention to broader political and social institutions and organizations. To introduce the element of subjective identity, Scott makes a similar claim: she states her agreement with "Rubin's formulation that psychoanalysis offers an important theory about the reproduction of gender, a description of the 'transformation of the biological sexuality of individuals as they are enculturated.'" (44). However, Scott rejects what she interprets as a "universal claim of psychoanalysis." What Scott finds useful is the way Lacanian theory enables reflection on the construction of gendered identities. What she considers problematic for historical research is that "If gender identity is based only and universally on fear of castration, the point of historical inquiry is denied." (44) As in the third element, Scott stresses that "Historians need instead to examine the ways in which gendered identities are substantively constructed and relate their findings to a range of activities, social organizations, and historically specific cultural representations" (44).

To illustrate the way that Scott's theory critically reconsiders the previous work on gender, let us compare its first part with Rubin's notion and with the definition of gender presented by Sandra Harding in a book published the same year (1986). In Rubin's case, Scott incorporates a consideration of the economic aspects and kinship structures in the third subset, and Rubin's appeal to the psychic production of girls and boys is present in the fourth element. However, we could also consider this last element of Rubin's perspective as related to the first and second subset if we think of the analysis of the phallus in

Freudian and Lacanian psychoanalysis as a culturally available symbol, on one hand, and if we consider the authority of psychoanalytic discourse itself as responsible of producing normative concepts of femininity and masculinity, on the other. Rubin's critical engagement with psychoanalysis had already pointed out that.

In Harding's case, she claimed that gendered social life is produced through three distinct processes that she names gender symbolism, gender structure (or the division of labor by gender), and individual gender. The first "is the result of assigning dualistic gender metaphors to various perceived dichotomies that rarely have anything to do with sex differences"; the second is "the consequence of appealing to these gender dualisms to organize social activity, of dividing necessary social activities between different groups of humans"; and the third "is a form of socially constructed individual identity only imperfectly correlated with either the 'reality' or the perception of sex differences" (17–18). Harding adds that gender appears only in culturally specific forms: "The referents for all three meanings of masculinity and femininity differ from culture to culture, though within any culture the three forms of gender are related to each other" (18).

Here, we can also identify a partial coincidence: both definitions share the consideration of symbols, economic or institutional division of roles or activities, and individual identity. Harding also stresses the interrelation between these aspects. However, Scott's specific poststructuralist perspective is evident in the presentation of not three but four aspects, specifically in the second one that condenses the view on language, power, and historical writing she is expressly endorsing with her theory. That is also why we understand the need for Scott to articulate her more sophisticated version of what has been the general definition of gender elaborated since the mid seventies with the second proposition that relates it to power and language: "gender is a primary field within which or by means of which power is articulated" (Scott 1999, 45). Scott clarifies that gender is not the only field – class and race would be relevant to, of course – but "it seems to have been a persistent and recurrent way of enabling the signification of power in the West, in the Judeo-Christian as well as Islamic tradition" (45). I will elaborate further on the relationship between discourse and power in Scott's perspective below, but before let us present her second proposition through the words of Smith (2013):

> Scott explained that gender could be a category or subject of discussion through which power operated. It could operate thus in several ways. For one, because gender meant differentiation, it could be used to distinguish the better from the worse, the more important from the less important. Using the term 'feminine' articulated a lower place in a social or political hierarchy no

matter what the term referred to. Gender explained or assigned meaning to any number of phenomena, including work, the body, sexuality, politics, religion, cultural production, and an infinite number of other terms. As such, phenomena were coded male or female, or as debates within these fields deployed categories of masculinity and femininity, power was at work. Thus, thinking about gender was a way to think about power, whether in society or in politics (90–91).

Smith highlights Foucault's influence in Scott given that his theory of power allowed her to introduce gender issues in political history "because gender itself was a form of power derived from creating and manipulating binary differences – primary among these being the difference that created men and women." (90).

Insofar as the first proposition critically gathers results from previous theorizations, the original contribution of Scott's theory lies in identifying the legitimating function of gender and the different ways in which it works. However, already in its second subset, her view of discourse and power was at work since Scott had already claimed there that historical inquiry on gender should trace the way that normative concepts of gender were established to secure a fixity that historians should always distrust. This is clear when Scott clarifies (in relation to the legitimating function of gender) that conceptual languages employ differentiation to establish meaning and "sexual difference is a primary way of signifying differentiation" (1999, 45). Scott says that she is advocating for a poststructuralist historical analysis since "post-structuralists do not fix a universal meaning for the categories or the relationship between them (...)" (233, n. 46). Scott concludes the presentation of her definition claiming that gender provides a way to decode meaning and to understand the complex connections among various forms of human interaction. Her argument about the way to theorize gender is, at the same time, an argument on how to historicize it: "When historians look for ways in which the concept of gender legitimizes and constructs social relationships, they develop insight into the reciprocal nature of gender and society and into the particular and contextually specific ways in which politics constructs gender and gender constructs politics" (46).

But we could ask, how does poststructuralist historical analysis work?

Poststructuralism and Feminist History: The Rise and the Fall of Gender?

Scott describes poststructuralist theories on knowledge as promising for historical studies in the introduction of the 1988 edition of *Gender and the Politics of History* (1999, 1–11). In effect, Scott's theorization of gender is a paradigmatic example of the impact that the work of Foucault and Derrida had during the eighties in the humanities at large.

What is key for our aim of reconstructing the emergence of the category is that gender, under poststructuralist eyes, is considered "the social organization of sexual difference" and "the knowledge that establishes meanings for bodily difference" (2). This definition is possible because, following Foucault, Scott considers knowledge as inseparable from social organization: in other words, intimately linked to politics as "power relationships."[8] Now, we can comprehend Scott's claim that there is a reciprocal nature of gender and society.

More specifically, Scott found in poststructuralism a perspective that made possible the inquiry into "how gender hierarchies are constituted, legitimated, challenged and maintained" (3) and gave her also a chance to study discrimination as something that extended to the categories of identities themselves. In this way, Scott believed that her critical drive as a feminist historian would be better served: that of pointing out and changing the inequalities between women and men and other groups left out of history.

To put forward such inquiry, it was necessary to question one assumption: the idea that categories of identity reflect the objective experience of those described by them. In the case of women, this also implied that the term "women" referred to an "objective identity" and that there were some inherent characteristics that defined women universally. This has clearly been one of the more debatable issues in feminist theory and politics throughout its history. Scott's theorization was built upon a rejection of such assumption insofar as it reinforced the idea of an inalterable sexual difference and, thus, "confirmed rather that challenge the prevailing (discriminatory) visions about women" (4).

In sum, one major tenet of Scott's theorization has been that no category of identity should be taken as self-evident and that even those basic terms we used to "merely describe" social groups must be historicized. Scott's work will insist on this poststructuralist approach throughout her writings: "that categories of identity we take for granted as rooted in our physical bodies (gender and race) or our cultural (ethnic, religious) heritages are, in fact, retrospectively linked to those roots; they don't follow predictably or naturally from them" (2011, 46).

Categories change, too, not just their historical circumstances. Knowledge of gender relates to gender power relations and vice versa. There is no pre-discursive experience as a bedrock of identity, and the meanings of identity categories are historical too.[9] In a way that resounds with Foucault's famous

---

[8] Scott also claims that knowledge is "relative" but I will comment on this later.
[9] Scott (1991) is also famous for her radical critique of the notion of experience both in conventional historiography and in its use by oppositional histories of difference in the eighties. I will not present her arguments here, although they are implicit in the reconstruction I am offering. For

claim in his writings on genealogy, Scott claims that "Nothing about the body, including women's reproductive organs, determines universally how social difference will be shaped" (1999, 2).

Two more elements are part of a poststructuralist historical analysis: a nonunilinear notion of causality and a theory on how meaning works. In relation to the first, Scott explains:

> Experience is not seen as the objective circumstances that condition identity; identity is not an objectively determined sense of self defined by needs and interests; politics is not the collective coming to consciousness of similarly situated individual subjects. Rather politics is the process by which plays of power and knowledge constitute identity and experience (5).

We understand now that categories of identity should always be historicized because identity and experience "are variable phenomena discursively organized in particular contexts or configurations" (5). But this does not imply positing another unilineal direction of causality, that of discourse "causing" experience and identity: the multicausal and mutual constitution of knowledge/politics and experience/identity should be the object of study of the historian.

Finally, Scott highlights poststructuralism's take on meaning insofar as it offers "a distinctive way of studying it in their emphasis on its variability, its volatility, and the political nature of its construction." (5) Scott explains:

> If the meanings of concepts are taken to be unstable, open to contest and redefinition, then they require vigilant repetition, reassertion, and implementation by those who have endorsed one or another definition. Instead of attributing a transparent and shared meaning to cultural concepts, poststructuralists insist that meanings are not fixed in a culture's lexicon but are rather dynamic, always potentially in flux (5).

This view demands the historian to trace exactly what Scott theorizes as the production of meaning in the relationship between symbols and normative concepts in her definition of gender:

> Their study therefore calls for attention to the conflictual processes that establish meanings, to the ways in which such concepts as gender acquire the appearance of fixity, to the challenges posed for normative social definitions, and to the ways these challenges are met – in other words, to the play of force involve in any society's construction and implementation of meanings: to politics (5).

---

such reconstruction, see La Greca (2023). For the impact of Scott's critique on gender history, see Berger (2022, 124–125).

According to Scott, this theoretical perspective allows historians in general, but feminist ones in particular, to interpret the world while trying to change it because it makes critical thinking of the past and the present a continuous operation. On one hand, feminist politics and academic studies of gender are considered part of "the same political project: a collective attempt to confront and change existing distributions of power" (6). On the other hand, it is, for Scott, a new way of thinking about history. First, because it demands that all categories be historicized, especially those that have seemed to be self-evident and basic vocabulary, such as "women" and "men." Gender, thus, should be studied "concretely and in context" as a "historical phenomenon, produced, reproduced, and transformed in different situations and over time" (6). How does this translate into historical research? Scott explains that we cannot tell a story of the things that happen to women and men and how they reacted to them: as we have said, the very meaning of "women" and "men" becomes an object of study. The historical question should be *how the subjective and collective meanings of women and men as categories of identity have been constructed?*

Second, it rejects "the compartmentalizing tendency" in social history that, until then, had relegated sex and gender to the institution of the family. Scott has argued that gender is an aspect of social organization generally: if the meanings of sexual difference are invoked and contested as part of many kinds of struggles for power, "Social and cultural knowledge about sexual difference is therefore produced in the course of most of the events and processes studied as history" (6).

Although Scott's work is considered a fundamental argument over the usefulness of gender for historical studies, I have said in the introduction that this Element also presents a narrative of the rise and fall of the category of gender. If its emergence in the seventies was a hallmark of the feminist reflection of that time and achieved the establishment of gender studies as a prominent interdisciplinary field during the eighties, towards the end of the decade, several critiques would undermine its status.

What seems paradoxical is that strong criticism will come from two key theorists of gender: Rubin and Scott. In "Thinking Sex: Notes for a Radical Theory of the Politics of Sexuality" (1984), Rubin argued that the focus on gender had accompanied a conservative drift of the feminist movement. More importantly, Rubin considered that gender justice was not equivalent to erotic justice. Thus, she concluded that feminism lacked a radical theory of sexuality that would not be produced by continuing research on gender issues.[10]

---

[10] In the nineties, Rubin will be considered a pioneer of sexualities and queer studies.

As I mentioned in the introduction, Scott will also doubt the usefulness of gender in the 1999 preface to the revised edition of her 1988 book. There, Scott believes that the development of gender studies and history ended up normalizing a notion that was proposed by feminist theorists to provoke disruption and destabilize theoretical and political discourse. Scott literally claims that gender as a category has lost its critical edge (as illustrated with the 1995 ONU conference anecdote) and, for that reason, she decided to use it less and less in her writings, "talking instead about differences between the sexes and about sex as a historically variable concept" (1999, xii). A new chapter added to the 1999 edition testifies about Scott's dissatisfaction with the uses and limits of gender. Claiming that feminist theory has always refused to accommodate the status quo, Scott concludes that: "we need to keep renewing our analytical vocabulary, even as we pay tribute to the critical work done by a term like 'gender' *for a brief moment* in our recent history" (xiii – my emphasis).

It seems that Scott moves too quickly from a celebration to a farewell of gender as an analytical category. However, she is a privileged witness to the strong criticism that the notion endured by the end of the eighties and into the next decade. Judith Butler's *Gender Trouble* would be a fundamental turning point in the theorization of gender (Scott 2011, 7). The following section will show how gender is critically examined not only in its relation to other features of identity but also in its very theoretical definition. Could it be that after arguing at large on our need to avoid taking any category of identity for granted, something about gender was left unhistoricized?

3 The Historicity of Gender: Knowledge, Power, and Bodies

In this section, I will present the severe criticism gender underwent within feminist theory debates since the late eighties and nineties that explains the seemingly tragic narrative presented in the previous section. However, instead of subscribing that narrative, I will underscore the critical gain that feminist theory achieved through these debates to offer an alternative interpretation of this theoretical process as a refiguration of gender as a *historical* category.

I will first present the critical work of black feminist thinkers and intersectional studies that pointed out the need to revise race blind spots in analyses of the sex-gender system. Then, I will reconstruct the theory of gender performativity by Judith Butler and its critique of the binary and heterosexist assumptions left unquestioned in the original definition of gender. I will supplement Butler's insights with Donna Haraway's reflection on situated knowledges to comprehend the relationship between knowledge and power, bodies and meanings. Butler's and Haraway's reflections will lead to a nuance understanding of the idea of gender as a social construction and to its refiguration as a historical category.

The final part of this section will also present a map of new academic fields that since the nineties intersected polemically with sex-gender research and contributed to its critical reconsideration. Thus, this Element will reconnect the theoretical reconstruction of the critiques to the concept of gender with its epistemic and political relevance in current public debates.

Gender under Question

The main critiques to the definition of gender are due to the very success of the scientific production of gender studies: to the extent that debates became more nuanced and complex, exploring further features of the experiences of femininity and masculinity feminist theorists faced challenges to the very theoretical design of the notion.

In general terms, critiques aimed to unacknowledged biases in the way that gender has been defined or used as an analytical category. Again, we found the intimate relation between the knowledge and the politics of bodies. This relationship has two sides: on the one hand, gender studies and feminist theory and history (as other approaches later to be called sexualities, intersectional, queer, and trans studies, for example) have been characterized by their critical drive both towards society and other disciplines assumptions that contributed to an unequal and unjust perspective on different groups or identities, and towards the reproduction of those same biases within academic production. Women, gender, and feminist studies were born thanks to the women's liberation movement of the sixties and shared its aim of ending sexism in society. This implied that all knowledge claims, disciplines, social practices, and institutions could be subjected to feminist criticism (as we saw with the elements that Scott's definition considered relevant to map how gender and its asymmetry of power worked).

On the other hand, the close relation between knowledge and power in gender studies and feminist theory and history relates to the acknowledgment of the positionality of those undertaking this line of research: an ethical drive that searches for the promotion of knowledges for a more equal social world. But this also implied that feminist research should remain vigilant concerning the reinforcement of other biases in its own work. Class and race issues have also been part of feminist inquiries in a complex relationship with issues of gender.

Taking into consideration the critical and ethical side of feminist's projects for tracing the knowledge and power of bodies, I will present the main critiques to the notion of gender in the late eighties and beginning of the nineties.

The Contribution of Black Feminism

Towards the end of the eighties, substantial challenges appeared to the notion of gender, echoing the debates that took place within the feminist movement. Among these criticisms, those of black and lesbian feminists stand out: they questioned the priority given to the category of gender over other identity features such as class, sexual orientation, race, or ethnicity (hooks 1984; Wittig 1992). As we have seen, "gender" aimed to move research beyond its reduction to the scope of "women" as an autonomous and/or universal classification. However, the central issue of these critiques was not solely the diversity of experiences that women can have, but more importantly, how these experiences are intersected by identity axes that overlap in complex ways. Furthermore, the suspicion expressed by different feminist thinkers and activists was: if gender is considered the main category of analysis, what other features of women's experiences are thus neglected or even made invisible? What relationship may this have with the reproduction of unequal power relations within women as a group?

bell hooks's key contribution challenged the place of gender as the primary category of analysis in feminist theory. In *Feminist Theory from Margin to Center* (1984), hooks articulates the demand of hearing the voice of black women not just in society as a whole but within the feminist movement and academia. hooks criticizes the focus on issues of gender by white feminist theorists insofar as it makes invisible or straightforwardly ignores issues of class and race that are equally relevant to understanding the different ways women experience oppression. In her words: "Privileged feminists have largely been unable to speak to, with, and for diverse groups of women because they either do not understand fully the *inter-relatedness of sex, race, and class oppression* or refuse to take this inter-relatedness seriously" (1984, 14 [my emphasis]).

hooks claims that it is misleading to focus exclusively on gender: to consider it the primary category to understand women's oppression evinces that those undertaking research are not considering that race or class have an equally relevant role as axes of domination. In simpler terms, the most prominent research in gender studies has been carried out by white feminists who do not acknowledge their own privileged position in a racist society: race does not figure as relevant in their work, given that their own experiences are not marked by racism as it is the case with black women. Hence, the issue of race is not properly considered in their theorizations. However, hooks does not claim that feminist research should be dismissed, given that it has been conducted in a biased form. On the contrary, hooks criticizes this racial blind spot to argue that black feminists have a key role in the general theoretical and political project of feminism.

Given that gender implies a relational understanding of femininity and masculinity, hooks explains how race illuminates in a particular way the experiences of black women in their relation to white women and to black men: black women share with white women the experience of sexist oppression. However, in terms of race, black women are oppressed while white women are privileged, and hence, participate in their oppression. Regarding black men, black women share with them the oppression due to a white supremacist organization of society, but in terms of gender, black men enjoy a privileged position in relation to black women. hooks concludes:

> White women and black men have it both ways. They can act as oppressor or be oppressed. (...) Both groups have led liberation movements that favor their interests and support the continued oppression of other groups. Black male sexism has undermined struggles to eradicate racism just as white female racism undermines feminist struggle. (...) Black women with no institutionalized "other" that we may discriminate against, exploit, or oppress often have a lived experience that directly challenges the prevailing classist, sexist, racist social structure and its concomitant ideology. This lived experience may shape our consciousness in such a way that our world view differs from those who have a degree of privilege (however relative within the existing system) (14–15).

The special vantage point that hooks believes black women occupy because of their marginal position in society implies a specific standpoint from which feminist theory could be better developed, avoiding its racial blind spot and incorporating a wider perspective on women's and men's specific experiences.[11] That is why hooks has been considered as part of the tradition of feminist standpoint theory, along with theorists such as Sandra Harding and Donna Haraway (Harding 2004).

Haraway (1991) highlights the relevance of the criticism women of color have offered of the "ethnocentric and imperializing tendencies of European and Euro-American feminisms," particularly since they started to publish in the early 1980s. Moreover, Haraway adds:

> US 'women of colour', itself a complex and contested political construction of sexed identities, produced critical theory about the production of systems of hierarchical differences, in which race, nationality, sex, and class were intertwined, both in the nineteenth and early twentieth century and from the earliest days of the women's movements that emerged from the 1960's civil rights and anti-war movements (144).

---

[11] For hooks influence in historiography, see Riley (2025).

As we saw, Lévi-Strauss's theory of the exchange of women in patriarchal societies to secure social relationality between men was used by Rubin to analyze how women were constituted as objects but not subjects of rights since they could be exchanged by their fathers in marriage. To give an example of how black feminist criticism illuminates the limits of this original theorization, Haraway explains that in the New World, black women were not constituted as 'woman', as white women were:

> Instead, black women were constituted simultaneously racially and sexually – as marked female (animal, sexualized and without rights), but not as woman (human, potential wife, conduit for the name of the father) – in a specific institution, slavery, that excluded them from "culture" defined as the circulation of signs through the system of marriage (145).

By presenting the incest taboo as a determinant of the passage from nature to culture, Lévi-Strauss's anthropology understood the specificity of "humanity" as related to kinship and the emergence of culture. However, as Haraway relates, not "every" body was considered "human" to the same extent. Within these implicit "degrees" of humanity, slavery condemned some bodies to the lesser status of "animal."

In Rubin's theory, kinship vested men with rights in women that they did not have in themselves. This explained the transformation of females into oppressed women, the cultural production of gender from "natural" sex. Rubin's anthropological perspective made clear how women's oppression was not a natural or necessary outcome, but a historically specific process. However, as hooks, Haraway, and others showed, "slavery abolished kinship for one group in a legal discourse that produced whole groups of people as alienable property" (Spillers quoted in Haraway 1991, 145).

In conclusion, the experience of black women cannot be separated from the institution of slavery since they were "unpositioned, unfixed, in a system of names; they were, specifically, unlocatable and so disposable" (Haraway 1991, 145). In other words, if white women "were not legally or symbolically *fully* human," slaves were "not legally or symbolically human *at all*" (146).

With hooks and Haraway, we also see that the issue of race relates not only to the history of slavery and its effects but also to the history of colonization. In "Moments of Danger: Race, Gender, and Memories of Empire" (1992), Vron Ware argues for a feminist theory of history that investigates the construction and reproduction of racialized femininities. Through a discussion of oral history, Ware considers how social memory of the British Empire "is continually affected and transformed by cultural forms in the present" (116). Her concern in this paper is "to understand how categories of racial, ethnic, and cultural difference – particularly between women – have been constructed in the past, in order to explore how these categories continue to be reproduced in more recent political and ideological conflicts" (116).

As hooks had already shown, Ware, too, stresses that, although feminism was supposed to appeal to women everywhere, "too many women have been excluded or left by the wayside feeling unwelcome, invisible, and unaccounted for by the representation of a sisterhood which was apparently 'white'" (119). Ware adds that it was not only "race" that divided women "but it has certainly presented feminists with one of the most complex puzzles" (119). Hence, Ware claims that any feminist historian wanting to adopt a perspective on race and gender ought to follow the model of black feminist criticism (120–121). Doing so would mean understanding that race is not a matter of exclusive concern to black people and that historical research should inquire into the social construction of whiteness. Here, Ware's argument resounds with Scott's perspective on historical analysis:

> In my view, an examination of the construction of whiteness, and in particular white femininity, can shift these debates away from an obsession with difference towards the less fashionable concept of *relational connectedness* [my emphasis]. For ideas about what constitutes white femininity are constructed in relation to those about black femininity, and vice versa. The different elements in this system of race and gender identity have no intrinsic meaning. They work only in and through differentiation. Furthermore, the task of uncovering and making connections between these different constructions may lead to a more useful understanding of the social relations of both race and gender (119–120).

Ware also argues for a similar relationship between knowledge and power in historical writing: "In order to figure out how ideas about black and white femininity are expressed today, it helps to consider how these categories have been produced historically" (199).

The value of black feminist criticism to feminist theory and historical writing is not reduced to showing the limits of an exclusive focus on gender and the complexity or "puzzles" when approaching the different experiences of femininity, masculinity, and oppression: it is to be found also in the answer that they provide, namely, the acknowledgement of the interrelatedness (as hooks claimed) or relational connectedness (in Ware's words) of gender, class, and race. It is to black feminist activism and theory that we owe the notion of *intersectionality*.

In the early nineties, Kimberlé Crenshaw (1991) published a groundbreaking article in which she used the term "intersectionality" as a metaphor to characterize how systems of oppression, such as gender and race overlap. As Patricia Hill Collins (2019) reconstructs:

> For Crenshaw, intersectionality named the structural convergence among intersecting systems of power that created blind spots in antiracist and feminist activism. Crenshaw counseled that antiracist and feminist movements would be compromised as long as they saw their struggles as separate and not intertwined. Significantly, racism and sexism not only fostered social inequalities, they marginalized individuals and groups that did not fit comfortably within race-only, gender-only mono-categorical frameworks (26).

Intersectional studies will develop in the following decades, retaining this critical insight. Black feminist contributions show that the development of the notion of gender has been motivated and challenged by social activism and its own debates. Thus, academics and activists have shared an interest in comprehending the puzzles of identity, among them the complex overlapping and sometimes opposing dynamics of issues of "gender" and "race."[12]

Judith Butler: Imploding the Sex/Gender Distinction

In *Gender Trouble* (1990), Butler undertakes a genealogical critique of gender as part of the basic vocabulary of the tradition of feminist theory.[13] Their critique aims at the very definition of the term as discontinuous from the notion of sex: that what we consider that pertains to gender does not "follow from" what sex is. This was the theoretical move that allowed feminists in the seventies to reject the idea that inequalities between men and women were justified in nature or biology: gender then "is neither the causal result of sex nor as seemingly fixed as sex" (1990, 8). However, as Butler explains:

---

[12] Laura Lee Downs testifies on the relevance of black feminist reflections to historical writing by claiming that "Good scholarship in gender history is therefore grounded in the practice of intersectionality, that is, in the idea that one must understand women and men as individuals who stand at the confluence of multiple social forces" (2019, 102). Downs explains that intersectionality assumed in the nineties "primacy of place in many historians' toolkits" (2019, 102) but adds that it should be considered "less a tool of analysis than a declaration of good practice. For affirming that individual identities are multiple and mutable, while an important step forward, tells us nothing about the ways that different shards of identity, such as race, gender, or ethnicity, articulate with class to form structures that are simultaneously classed, raced, and gendered. Only detailed historical or sociological research can lay bare the particular shape assumed by those articulations at any given place or moment in time." (107) Downs comments on Garthine Walker's research on the complex and variable emotional responses to child-killing in sixteenth- to eighteenth-century Britain as an intersectional historical inquiry into the subjectivities of the accused women (110–114). Berger also stresses how the concept of intersectionality influenced gender history (2022, 121). As examples of historical works that apply an intersectional perspective, Berger refers to the work of Alice Kessler-Harris, Lynn M. Thomas, Kathryn Burns, and Lata Mani (2022, 121). For the relevance of an intersectional approach to the history of sexualities, see Weeks 2016, 58.

[13] Butler prefers they/them pronouns.

> Taken to its logical limit, the sex/gender distinction suggests a radical discontinuity between sexed bodies and culturally constructed genders. Assuming for the moment the stability of binary sex, it does not follow that the construction of "men" will accrue exclusively to the bodies of males or that "women" will interpret only female bodies. Further, even if sexes appear to be unproblematically binary in their morphology and constitution (which will become a question), there is no reason to assume that genders ought also to remain as two (9).

Although feminist theorists had already argued that what has been considered feminine and masculine had no necessary relation with the way bodies are sexed, Butler is pointing out that a certain continuity between the categories remained implicit: insofar as what is feminine is considered as the cultural meaning of female bodies, and what is masculine, of male bodies. But, if there is a discontinuity, why has this correspondence been preserved? Moreover, why claim that there are two genders for two sexes, and not three, four or any other number? Butler concludes that: "The presumption of a binary gender system implicitly retains the belief in a mimetic relation of gender to sex whereby gender mirrors sex or is otherwise restricted by it" (9). Hence, if gender is to be fully considered as constructed and radically independent of sex, "*man* and *masculine* might just as easily signify the female body as a male one, and *woman* and *feminine* a male body as easily as a female one" (9).[14]

The resistance of our gendered "common sense" to accept this claim is proof of Butler's point: that there is an unjustified assumption of correspondence or correlation between sex and gender that remains in place in the feminist theorization of gender. However, Butler's argument goes even deeper: they also pose questions over the supposed "natural" or "given" status of sex:

> Can we refer to a "given" sex or a "given" gender without first inquiring into how sex and/or gender is given, through what means? And what is "sex" anyway? Is it natural, anatomical, chromosomal, or hormonal, and how is a feminist critic to assess the scientific discourses which purport to establish such "facts" for us? Does sex have a history? (9)

Butler claims that what we consider "sex" is also culturally constructed insofar as it depends on scientific and institutional discourses. In other words, the meanings of "sex" are historical, too. If this is so, then "sex" is not a pre-discursive reality. Moreover, Butler will also conclude that it is our understanding of gender that produces our idea of sex as a fixed binary: the notion of sex is not the cause of gender – we already knew that – but an effect of gender. This is more difficult to grasp or accept: "If the immutable character of sex is contested,

---

[14] Jack Halberstam (1998) studies female masculinity.

perhaps this construct called 'sex' is as culturally constructed as gender; indeed, perhaps it was always already gender, with the consequence that the distinction between sex and gender turns out to be no distinction at all" (9–10).

Here is Butler's most polemical claim that amounts to a strong blow to the very category that previous feminist theorists championed during the eighties. Paradoxically, we could use Scott's own words to understand Butler's critique: *gender is a primary field within which or by means of which power is articulated*. Butler's argument traces how this legitimating function of gender works even at the level of the determination of what sex is. It is the sex binary that remained unchallenged in the original definition of gender, even in Scott's own theorization, as she would recognize in her writings from the nineties.

While black feminists and the notion of intersectionality questioned the exclusive relevance or priority of gender when studying the oppressed experience of women, Butler's *Gender Trouble* represents the climax of the tragic narrative of the emergence of the category of gender insofar as it attacks its very definition: they question its theoretical heart, the analogy that sex is to nature as gender is to culture. This founding analogy makes nature (and the body understood as natural) a mere passivity that receives the active imposition of form from culture.[15] However, Butler not only distrusts the notions of nature and culture that the parallelism presupposes: but they also undermine the analogy by questioning its theoretical performance and its political effects. If we take the sex-gender distinction to its limit as a distinction between the natural-given-prediscursive and the cultural-constructed-discursive, in their own words:

> It would make no sense, then, to define gender, as the cultural interpretation of sex, if sex itself is a gendered category. Gender ought not to be conceived merely as the cultural inscription of meaning on a pregiven sex (a juridical conception): gender must also designate the very apparatus of production whereby the sexes themselves are established. As a result, gender is not to culture as sex is to nature; gender is also the discursive/cultural means by which "sexed nature" or "natural sex" is produced and established as "prediscursive", prior to culture, a politically neutral surface *on which* culture acts (10).

To this extent, the original definition of gender has been seriously undermined even in its most sophisticated version. This critique of gender is also not just a "theoretical" one: it goes hand in hand with a critique of the political limits of the way feminist theory had understood gender. The target of Butler's critique is the heterosexist assumptions behind the notion and its presupposition of ideal

---

[15] Butler is building their argument on previous critiques of this dichotomy by feminist epistemologists such as Harding and Haraway.

sexual dimorphism. Moreover, Butler claims that the heterosexual matrix through which subjects are formed as gendered subjects requires that the binary of sex be posited as prediscursive: it is because we believe that the zero degree of embodiment is exhausted by the options of "male" or "female" and their corresponding "masculine" or "feminine" gender that heterosexuality as a social norm is sustained, reproduced, and reinforced.

Here we also have a reversal or denial of the presupposition of a linear nature of the relationship between sex, gender, and desire: even in the definition of gender, there was an assumption that "first there was sex," as the given *nature* of bodies, male and female (a reality outside time, history and interpretation); then "there was gender," as the *historical* interpretation of male and female bodies as men and women and their roles, rights, or possibilities in society; and because of that, "finally" we have heterosexual desire as the erotic and affective *destiny* of human males and females. This linearity is criticized because it lacks justification: it is supported by a metaphysical or foundational view of the nature of human bodies or "nature" itself, on the one hand, and it also assumes that history, as the realm of human development, is linear in itself, positing an "origin" that explains why what comes later has happened, and even a teleological drive, where the aim of human relationality is heterosexuality. History would then come "after" nature (as in Lévi-Strauss's anthropology), and the temporal process of "humanization" would be, at the same time, a departure from our animal origin and delimited or confined by our natural instincts toward reproduction, understood in its cultural form as heterosexuality.

These foundational, linear, and teleological assumptions had already been challenged by poststructuralism, as we saw with Scott. These assumptions are also rejected in Butler's text, given that Butler is presenting a genealogical critique of gender. There is no "origin" to reconstruct, no time "before oppression" – as the theories of patriarchy or even Rubin's sex-gender system implied. As Butler would famously claim, there is no original "man" and "woman" for which other forms of embodiment – lesbian, gay, trans, or nonbinary – would be derivative copies or abnormal forms. Thus, a poststructuralist critique focuses on the regime of knowledge-power that requires that narrative of origin to reproduce itself. Butler calls it "heterosexual matrix":

> I use the term *heterosexual matrix* throughout the text to designate that grid of cultural intelligibility through which bodies, genders, and desires are naturalized. I am drawing from Monique Wittig's notion of the "heterosexual contract" and, to a lesser extent, on Adrienne Rich's notion of "compulsory heterosexuality" to characterize a hegemonic discursive/epistemic model of gender intelligibility that assumes that for bodies to cohere and make sense there must be a stable sex expressed through a stable gender (masculine

expresses male, feminine expresses female) that is oppositionally and hierarchically defined through the compulsory practice of heterosexuality (208, n. 6).

This notion attests to the primacy given by Butler to compulsive or normative heterosexuality as a fundamental norm in Western culture. Butler is following Foucault's take on *The History of Sexuality* (1980) and building their theory from lesbian critical interventions within the feminist movement and from the previous theoretical work by lesbian feminists such as Monique Wittig, Adrienne Rich, and, of course, Rubin (1975) who had already argued that the incest taboo presupposed another, more fundamental taboo on homosexuality. Moreover, Rubin (1984) also studied the normative and oppressive aspects of our understanding of sexuality. However, there is another contextual element that influences Butler's take on compulsory heterosexuality: the HIV/AIDS crisis since the eighties and how it made visible the violent consequences of homophobia that prevented proper response to the epidemic all over the world (and, particularly, in the United States under Reagan's administration).

If our knowledge and experience of sex, gender, and desire are produced by a heterosexual matrix, this means that it is not because there are male and female humans that they are destined to love or desire in a heterosexual way (if they are to be considered "normal" subjects). Sexual dimorphism is not the cause of heterosexuality; it is the other way around. Heterosexuality is a social construction whose effect is our belief in sexual dimorphism as the uncontested given nature of bodies. If heterosexuality is the "natural" sexual orientation, homosexuality, then, is "unnatural," even a mental disease, as it was considered by the World Health Organization and psychiatric handbooks until 1990.

For the reader not familiar with feminist and queer theory developments of the last four decades, here again, they could find a counter-intuitive claim. Is Butler claiming that human bodies cannot be described as being either male or female? Yes, that is Butler's claim in part, but some clarifications are needed. On the one hand, Butler is not the first one to point this out. Previous studies on the history of science have contributed to the critique of sexual dimorphism and male and female as dichotomic or "opposed" to each other, as in the research by Foucault and Haraway. On the other hand, the sentence "human bodies cannot be described as being either male or female" is not the correct phrasing of Butler's claim: it should rather be "human bodies cannot be *neutrally* described as being either male or female." What I am highlighting is that it is not an issue of *impossibility* of description: it is an issue of *possibilities* of description and their consequences. What poststructuralism (and other linguistic turn perspectives) taught us is that a *neutral* description is impossible. Thus, we see again the intimate relation between knowledge and politics that is stressed by Butler in the same manner as in Scott's texts.

The explicit political aim of Butler's critique is the presence of a homophobic bias in gender studies and feminist theory. Butler's genealogical critique shows that what was left unquestioned in the sex-gender distinction had the political effect of securing heterosexual assumptions. Does this distinction make room for lesbian and gay ways of living one's embodiment? Are lesbians "other forms" of being a woman?[16] Are they derivative forms of an original one? Moreover, why did "woman" tacitly imply "heterosexual woman"? Is there a "normal" way of being a woman and an "abnormal" one? By building on Foucault's histories of the way that sciences and institutions since the seventeenth century focused on sexually so-called deviated or abnormal subjects, Butler shows that feminist theory – as society at large – uncritically assumed that heterosexuality is the norm for people's way of loving and desiring. In their argument, the unexamined assumption of the binary of gender and sexual dimorphism is the ungrounded ground on which that assumption rested and continued to be reproduced.[17]

So far, then, we have traced the following problematic assumptions of the analytical category of gender: (1) the sex-gender binarism by which women correspond to femininity and men to masculinity, which reinforces the matrix of compulsive heterosexuality, that is, the assumption that there are only two sexes, two corresponding genders and a sexual desire of one gender for the other; (2) the taboo of homosexuality, which made it impossible to consider nonheterosexual sexualities as modes of desire with equal legitimacy instead of seeing them as "deviant" forms; and (3) ideal sexual dimorphism: taking the heterosexual binary normative framework for granted reinforced the classification of the body as "either woman or man," with no third option. In this case, intersex activism has been fundamental, given that declaring "pathological" the anatomy of newborns who did not conform to ideal sexual dimorphism has resulted in the violence of surgical "correction" of their bodies to adjust to "what should have been the case" (Fausto-Sterling 2000).

Respectively, these cultural assumptions contributed to the reproduction of unjust social hierarchies and even violence toward: (1) trans and nonbinary, (2) gay and lesbian, and (3) intersex lives. The suspicion around the notion of

---

[16] Monique Wittig famously claimed that lesbians were not women since the normative sex-gender system defined the category of women as exclusively heterosexual.

[17] Along with Foucault's work, Berger claims that Butler's critique of the sex-gender distinction enabled the development of the field of history of sexualities (2022, 111). See also Weeks (2016, 50). Susan Stryker also acknowledges the relevance of Butler's work not only on trans studies and historiography but in trans activism as well (2008, 131).

gender was that it was part of the problem rather than part of the solution. Due to this criticism, Butler and Scott argued in their nineties' writings that feminist theoretical focus should move to issues of sex or sexual difference instead of issues of gender (Butler 1993; Scott 1999). Such claims make plausible to write a narrative of the "rise" and "fall" of the analytical category of gender as the result of these feminist debates.

Refiguring Gender as a Historical Category

As Hayden White (1987) has taught theorists of history, the need to establish *the* historical narrative of past occurrences only emerges in the face of at least two rival interpretations. So far, this essay has been presenting a narrative of the emergence, development, and "fall" of the category of gender within US feminist theory. The tragic emplotment of this story was plausible in the nineties because of the attitude change of two of the gender's major theorists: Gayle Rubin and Joan Scott. Both reconsidered their enthusiasm for the category in their classic pieces and expressed later that gender had shown limited success in its original aims or had even lost its critical edge. Scott moved on during the nineties to considerations of sexual difference and increasingly incorporated a psychoanalytical perspective for feminist history. In 2011, Scott presented an explicit narrative of criticism of her theorization of gender, although she reconsidered the notion in light of Freud's writings. In that narrative, Scott puts Butler's work as a critical turning point. In the case of Rubin, her research interest will move towards sexuality studies, more specifically, an anthropological inquiry into sexual communities, antipornographic politics, and BDSM practices.

However, in the very moment where the champions of gender are second-guessing their original positions and Butler is producing what seems the final stab at the notion of gender, we can offer another reading of what was happening from today's vantage point: rather than the definitive fall of gender as a useful analytical category, we see its redefinition as a *historical* one thanks to the critical consciousness produced by feminist debates over the limits and problems of the dichotomy it presupposed between sex and gender. Moreover, we can risk a historical hypothesis: where Scott saw proof of gender's loss of its critical edge – as we saw in the introduction, the controversy during the 1995 ONU Women Forum – we may now see instead the beginning of another episode of its destabilizing power, given that since then "gender" became the sign by which conservative groups will reject demands by women, feminist, and LGBTQI+ activist understood as a single whole. Paradoxically, while feminist debates increasingly questioned the usefulness of gender for theoretical research and political transformation, conservative groups started using "gender" (more recently, "gender ideology") as useful to encompass the "cause" of the social transformations, legislation, and policies in favor of women and LGBTQI+ people they opposed. This paradoxical iteration of the use of "gender" can be comprehended by tracing its historical redefinition in the previous debates.[18]

The Performativity of Gender

As with black feminist thought, Butler's contribution also offers a new way of thinking about gender, one that is built over the destructive power of their intervention. In addition to defining the knowledge-power dynamic through which subjects are gendered as a heterosexual matrix, Butler claims that gender should be redefined as *performative*. Why call it performative? Butler considers gender as related to the performative feature of discourse, its possibility of bringing about what it names.[19]

Although a thorough analysis exceeds this Element, let us recall Austin's famous distinction between a constative and a performative use of language. Austin showed that there are situations in which the words that are uttered do not "describe" what is happening but constitute what is happening. If I say: "This sentence is written in English," I am making a constative utterance whose aim is to describe an occurrence, and, hence, it makes sense to ask if what I said is true or false. However, when in the context of a marriage ceremony, a priest says, "I declare you husband and wife," he is not describing something that has already happened. He is not informing the audience of a "fact": he is actually joining two persons in marriage by saying those words. It is the same case when I make a promise: if I say, "I promise I will pay you my debt, I am not referring to an extralinguistic event that may make my sentence true or false. In fact, my words are not true or false because the performative use of language is not properly assessed in terms of truth conditions. My promise will be kept or broken, but it makes no sense to say it was true or false when I made it. It was made regardless of whether I kept it or not in the future.

Of course, some conditions must be met for the speech act to be valid: for example, the person performing the marriage should be the appropriate one, and the person must follow the conventions related to the act. Hence, the

---

[18] In other words, for current historical research, it can be useful to trace how the current moment of public discussions over gender may have one of its roots in the specific "furor" of 1995.
[19] Butler builds their view on performativity from John Austin's theory of speech acts and Derrida's deconstructive reading of Austin (see La Greca 2014). They also combine it with Foucault's history of sexuality and biopower.

performative use of language relates to norms and institutions that give it its force, its ability to be successful as an act or, as Austin preferred, to be felicitous.

Butler combines the idea of the performativity of language with Foucault's thesis on biopower; thus, the emergence of the subject is a process within a matrix of knowledge and power that produces it as a gendered subject. There is a performative declaration at the moment of birth, where the institutions of medicine and the law are involved, that produces subjects as "boys" or "girls." This production is not a single act; it is a process that goes on and is reiterated throughout people's lives under social surveillance. In a sense, the gender we are assigned at birth (and, with today's technologies, even before birth) is a promise society demands us to keep – a promise we were not really "there" as conscious subjects to make in the first place. That is the effect of the compulsory repetition of gender norms and the paradox of the subject, as Foucault has shown: we are enabled as subjects by social norms at the same time that we are "subjected" to them.

If gendered subjects are produced within a heterosexual matrix, then gender is an accomplishment, not an attribute that is merely "expressed" or the "cause" of how we behave, desire, or love. In Butler's words:

> If gender attributes and acts, the various ways in which a body shows or produces its cultural signification, are performative, then there is no preexisting identity by which an act or attribute might be measured; there would be no true or false, real or distorted acts of gender, and the postulation of a true gender identity would be revealed as a regulatory fiction. That gender reality is created through sustained social performances means that the very notions of an essential sex and a true or abiding masculinity or femininity are also constituted as part of the strategy that conceals gender's performative character and the performative possibilities for proliferating gender configurations outside the restricting frames of masculinist domination and compulsory heterosexuality (1990, 192–193).[20]

A key element of gender as performative is its rejection of the idea of a "preexisting identity." More specifically, Butler challenges the idea of a "cause" of our gendered self as a foundation that would universally define our experience and behavior as women or men. As genealogy reveals, it is the other way around: our self-perception as women or men is the effect of a series of compulsive behaviors we are obliged to repeat since birth. Gender is thus related to the social expectations around our way of living our embodiment.

Thinking of gender as performative means that it is an effect of normative discursive practices and frameworks that constitute us through the compulsive

---

[20] In the context of this quote, Butler is making a distinction between expressiveness and performativity. However, they will reconsider this distinction in later work (see Butler 2015).

repetition of those behaviors and roles: it is this repetition, sustained over time, that creates in us the illusory belief in being (or having to be) coherent subjects of sex, gender, and sexual desire, that is, of "having" a gendered "identity" in a substantial sense. As a process reiterated over time, gender is a social ritual drama that requires the performance to be repeated, rewarded, or punished. Bodies are no longer considered passive surfaces of cultural inscription but are seen as a sedimented effect of this process of compulsive repetition, as *bodily styles*.

Now, this constitution is contingent and not necessary in a philosophical sense: it could have been different. There is no metaphysical foundation that grounds and determines it. That is why there is a compulsion to repeat in order to approach the normative binary ideals of "true woman" and "true man." Moreover, since they are social ideal norms, they are impossible to fully embody. That is why Butler sees in the performativity of gender also a theory of agency: to the extent that repetition is understood as an iteration without an origin or foundation, it is then a temporal process subject to failure, to the possible displacement (and change) of gender norms.[21] As we saw, Butler claimed that believing in an essential sex or a true or abiding masculinity or femininity (or implicitly accepting this by not historicizing these notions) conceals the performativity of gender. However, if we see gender as performative, what gains "visibility" are *the possibilities for proliferating gender configurations outside the restricting frames of masculinist domination and compulsory heterosexuality*. In simpler terms, gay, lesbian, trans, intersex, and nonbinary modes of existence are subject positions produced by the same heterosexual binary matrix that produces "normal" straight women and men but given its normative nature, the former are socially read (and punished) as "not-normal."

We could say that the recognition of the hierarchical component implicit in the apparently "neutral" social classifications of bodies had already been made explicit and denounced through the notion of gender in the seventies and eighties, showing how the relational definition of masculinity and femininity established an asymmetry by which what was feminine was socially valued as inferior to what was masculine. In the performative conception, this implicit hierarchy is also criticized, but the binary reading of gender is rejected: now,

---

[21] This essay does not do justice to Butler's appeal to Derrida's work, specifically his notions of iterability and citationality. My presentation of the notion of performativity aims at introducing the impact of *Gender Trouble* in feminist theory. For a detailed understanding of Butler's evolving theorization of gender in relation to the materiality of sex or the psychic dimension of subjection, see Butler (1993, 1997, 2004, 2015, 2024). For a thorough assessment of the impact of Derrida on theory of history, see Kleinberg 2017.

what is made explicit is how the heterosexual matrix forces a dynamic of inferiorization between "normal" subject-bodies and those that will be read as deviant or pathological. That is why, in Butler's view, the force of the performative relates not only to biopower and its generative effects but also to the violence of gender norms that are policed in formal and informal ways. The interpretation of homosexual, transsexual, and gender nonconforming people as deviant or mentally ill enabled their criminalization, imprisonment, or seclusion in psychiatric institutions until quite recently.[22]

So far, I have presented Butler's take on gender to show that, although it was properly read in the nineties as a strong blow on the theorization produced by previous feminist theory, it also opened then the way for its critical refiguration. That is why I propose to abandon the seemingly tragic narrative of the "rise and fall" of the usefulness of gender and replace it with a different retrospective take from the vantage point of the present – a moment in which the meaning of gender is, again, openly contested. Hence, let me explain what it means to refigure gender as a historical category.

The theory of performativity refigures the category of gender as a historical one by casting gender in itself as a historical emergence or event (Scott 1991): its definition is the result of a specific context, with its specific possibilities and limits, its assumptions and biases, its power relations. It is also a temporal classification with no foundational status and can change or be redefined by being used and contested. When we considered gender as an analytical category, we had already claimed that it named the changing organization of sexual difference as a historical phenomenon. However, if it is a historical category, we can question the implicit binary understanding of its relationship to the notion of sex. The iterable nature of all categories, even those related to identity, gives us a key into their historicity:

> To understand gender as a historical category, however, is to accept that gender, understood as one way of culturally configuring the body, is open to a continual remaking, and that "anatomy" and "sex" are not without cultural framing (as the intersex movement has clearly shown). The very attribution of femininity to female bodies as if it were a natural or necessary property takes place within a normative framework in which the assignment of femininity to femaleness is one mechanism for the production of gender itself (Butler 2004, 9–10).

Gender, then, is both a cultural way of configuring the body and open to its remaking. This process of making and remaking what counts as a *legible* body relates to its historicity: "Terms such as 'masculine' and 'feminine' are

---

[22] Even today, there are countries with laws against homosexuality or trans people.

notoriously changeable; there are *social histories* for each term; their meaning change radically depending upon geopolitical boundaries and cultural constraints on who is imagining whom, and for what purpose" (10, my emphasis) The historicity of gender is also tied to a repetition open in its effects, its performativity:

> That the terms recur is interesting enough, but the recurrence does not index sameness, but rather the way in which the social articulation of the term depends upon its repetition, which constitutes one dimension of the performative structure of gender. Terms of gender designation are thus never settled once and for all but are constantly in the process of being remade (10).

Let me spell out some features of the historicity of gender: the embodied subject emerges through a temporal process that has no foundational origin that determines "from the start" what it will become and no closed destiny either. Hence, subjects are opened "at both ends" of their becoming: this openness explains the production of subjectivity through the forced repetition of ideal gender norms – because there is no given, preexisting identity – and the possibility of agency – because the singular process by which a body interacts with those norms combines ways of approximating them and ways of deviating or swerving from them.

There is another side of the openness of subjects that relates to gender as an enactment, a social ritual drama. Gender is lived as an internal reality, but feminist theorists have shown that it exceeds this reductive way of defining it – in another sense in which "the personal is political." Gender also relates to available symbols, normative concepts, and political, social, economic, and religious institutions and practices. It does not belong solely to the private sphere: it is also a very public issue, something that could be illustrated with nineteenth-century legislation on dress codes (e.g., see Stryker 2008).

Gender relates to knowledge and power, words and doings, and the private and public spheres. Given the changing nature of these realms, we encounter again what Scott had already stated regarding the task of the historian: to trace how concepts such as gender acquire the appearance of fixity and to pay attention to the play of force involved in any society's construction and implementation of meanings: to politics. This construction is also done through our knowledge practices. Again, knowledge and politics of bodies are intimately related. How can we, then, understand this relationship without collapsing one notion into the other? To answer this, I will introduce Haraway's notion of situated knowledges. With it, I will argue that an integral feature of the historical redefinition of gender is born from the way that feminist theory imploded another dualism, that between nature and culture that has been a founding assumption of the definition of gender as opposed to sex.

Donna Haraway's Situated Knowledges: History and Embodiment Beyond Dualisms

One of the theses that defined gender as a social construction presupposed that "sex" belongs to the realm of nature as the fixed and given "raw material" of embodiment. Butler's critique of the sex-gender distinction was influenced by feminist inquiries that had put that dualism into question. Donna Haraway's work has been key to rethinking the relationship between nature and culture, sex and gender, language and materiality, constructivism and empiricism, and, with that, knowledge and power. If performativity allows us to refigure gender as a historical category, the notion of situated knowledges is also fundamental for further elaborating on the relationship between the knowledge and politics of bodies this redefinition entails.

In "Situated Knowledges: The Science Question in Feminism and the Privilege of Partial Perspective," Haraway claims that:

> Gender is a field of structured and structuring difference, in which the tones of extreme localization, of the intimately personal and individualized body, vibrate in the same field with global high-tension emissions. Feminist embodiment, then, is not about fixed location in a reified body, female or otherwise, but about nodes in fields, inflections in orientations, and responsibility for difference in material-semiotic fields of meaning (1988, 588).

I want to highlight the partial coincidences of this definition with Scott's and Butler's ones. First, we have the notion of field. Second, we found the association of gender with the production of difference. Third, they reject the idea of "fixity" or "reification" in relation to embodiment. Haraway will also relate embodiment with a matrix, as we shall see later (595).

The idea of "nodes" in a field and responsibility "for difference" indicates the entanglement between a feminist perspective on embodiment and ethics. This is so because Haraway is elaborating the notion of situated knowledges as a feminist redefinition of scientific objectivity by which the intimate ties between bodies, knowledge, and power are acknowledged in their tension and potency.

Feminist epistemologists in the eighties rejected the definition of scientific objectivity as value neutrality for two interconnected reasons: first, because it presupposed an unattainable knowledge ideal and, second, because it had historically enabled a specific hegemonic perspective to be accepted as "the universal" scientific point of view. It is an impossible ideal because it presupposes a timeless, ahistorical, and unconditioned subject of knowledge: one that is nowhere and comes from nowhere. This is nothing other than the "God Trick": believing that we could know as a God would, who exists without being in any specific time and place and can see everything at once. However, in the history of modern science, as feminist epistemologists have shown, a specific subject position occupied "the" scientific position: that of the white, cis, heterosexual, bourgeois male.[23] Hence, the class, race, and gender biases of much of scientific production (Harding 1986). There has been then no real "value neutrality" in an epistemological sense. Moreover, the God Trick also leads to ethical shortcomings: by promising a perspective of transcendence of all limits, the modern notion of the objective subject fails to take responsibility for its knowledge claims.

For Haraway, the issue of the God Trick view of objectivity and the biases in scientific research that it made possible is not just a question of "bad science." Instead, it is a question of the need to redefine our understanding of the subject of knowledge.[24] The feminist reformulation of objectivity means recognizing that there is no subject without a body and, therefore, without location, without marks of gender, race, class, sexual orientation, and so on. We have mistakenly thought about what we do when we investigate and produce knowledge if we do not take seriously the embodied nature of our existence and our knowledge practices. Knowledge is a human activity, one that is, as we ourselves are, subject to change and finitude – as the philosophy, history and sociology of science have shown during the second half of the twentieth century.

Our embodied existence locates us in a time, a place and a series of social classifications or categories of identity. That is why objectivity cannot avoid recognizing the situated status of our knowledge practices and claims. Nevertheless, Haraway's idea of a subject of situated knowledges (in the plural) does not define this situatedness as a fixed location or close identity. On the contrary, similarly to Butler's performativity, it also reveals our openness and relationality. Redescribing scientific practice from a conception of the subject that recognizes its embodied self teaches us about the limits of knowledge as much as it illuminates our partial perspective and positioned rationality. Situationality is epistemological and political: partiality (and not universality) becomes the condition for being heard, for making rational affirmations, and for being held responsible.

Since Haraway's theoretical project has been to keep doing science, to produce "better accounts of the world," she offers a meaning of science "that

---

[23] For an explanation of the use of the term "cis" as different from "trans" see the brief introduction to trans studies next.
[24] See Smith (1992) and (1995) for similar critiques in the context of historiography.

insists on its potency in ideological struggles" (1988, 591): "Science has been utopian and visionary from the start: that is one reason 'we' need it" (585). This clarification relates to Haraway's interest in moving beyond the constructivist versus empiricist dichotomy in general epistemological discussions and within the feminist theory tradition. Objectivity as situated knowledges implies a rejection of relativism. Here we find a certain difference with Scott's and Butler's poststructuralist frameworks. It is mostly a difference in rhetoric, since Haraway shares the critical drive of semiology, deconstruction, poststructuralism, and narratology, but believes that we can still reclaim a notion of objective scientific knowledge. As she claims: "We need the power of modern critical theories of how meanings and bodies get made, not in order to deny meanings and bodies, but in order to build meanings and bodies that have a chance for life" (580).

Hence, objectivity as situated knowledges is not dichotomously opposed to value-neutrality. On the contrary, it is an attempt to move beyond sterile dichotomies like empiric-constructed, fact-fiction, and discovered-invented. For Haraway, in the objectivity-relativism dichotomy, both positions evade responsibility. The relativist "anything goes" that maintains that no objectivity is possible, that any position is equally valid, denies the relevance of critical research, and reduces the production of knowledge to a "mere" power game. For Haraway, we can recognize the mutual implications between power and knowledge without falling into the relativist extreme by engaging in "power-sensitive" conversations. In short, although modern science has fallen short of its emancipatory aims, it would be a mistake to see it as exclusively designed for oppression.

In sum, the voices of the oppressed are needed in science. If striving for situated knowledges means being accountable for our partial perspective, knowledge production needs to foster conversations between standpoints. To be "sensitive to power" means that we acknowledge that in the history of science, not every voice has been heard – as feminism itself has shown. Research must be undertaken recognizing the different power relations in which we participate. In sum, rationality is possible: it is redefined as critical positioning, as being accountable for our knowledge claims.

Since Haraway is moving beyond the empiricist-constructionist dichotomy, she frames the terms of the theoretical challenge as follows: how to have *simultaneously* an account of radical historical contingency for all knowledge claims and knowing subjects, a critical practice of recognizing our own "semiotic technologies" for making meanings, and a no-nonsense commitment to faithful accounts of the "real" world (579). It is clear that the first part of this sentence sums up Scott's poststructuralist take on history and gender.

The second part relates to the linguistic turn in general. Within contemporary theory of history, Hayden White's work (1973) has been a paradigmatic effort to recognize the way that historical writing appeals to figurative resources to "make meaning." White's take on historical writing is a sophisticated theory of how we make historical meaning. However, as Pihlainen (2017) has shown, discussions over White's contribution tended to arrive at sterile debates around the dichotomy of history as fact or fiction. Since the spirit of situated knowledges is to avoid such dualism, Haraway's take can be useful for the theory of history, too.

To further understand Haraway's position in relation to bodies, meaning, sex, and gender, we need to introduce another notion: that of the "material-semiotic actor." Haraway connects the redefinition of objectivity with the critique of the dichotomy between subject and object of knowledge that makes the first one the powerful agent that appropriates the latter, that uses it as a resource as if the object were a passive, inert entity. To reject these assumptions, Haraway offers the notion of "material-semiotic actor" that "is intended to portray the object of knowledge as an active, meaning-generating part of apparatus of bodily production, without ever implying the immediate presence of such objects or, what is the same thing, their final or unique determination of what can count as objective knowledge at a particular historical juncture" (1988, 595).

Haraway is inspired by Katie King's notion of "apparatus of literary production" understood as "a matrix from which literature" is born:

> Like "poems," which are sites of literary production where language too is an actor independent of intentions and authors, bodies as objects of knowledge are material-semiotic generative nodes. Their boundaries materialize in social interaction. Boundaries are drawn by mapping practices; "objects" do not preexist as such. Objects are boundary projects. But boundaries shift from within, boundaries are very tricky. What boundaries provisionally contain remains generative, productive of meanings and bodies (595).

Hence, objects of knowledge emerge at the intersection of different practices, among them, the views on the biological body that Haraway claims that emerged at the intersection of biological research and writing, medical and other business practices, and technologies (596).

To understand fully Haraway's concept (and its relevance in Butler's argument), let us present her critique of the sex-gender distinction. For Haraway, this distinction presented sex as "only the matter to the act of gender," where "Sex is 'resourced' for its representation as gender, which 'we' can control. It has seemed all but impossible to avoid the trap of an appropriationist logic of domination built into the nature/culture opposition and its generative lineage, including the sex-gender distinction" (592).

In effect, as we saw, the original definition of gender as cultural meant that it was subject to change, either over the course of history or by political action. And since this was connected to the feminist rejection of biological determinism, sex remained as "natural" or given. Haraway believes that, in the eighties' feminist debates, the notion of sex as an object of biological knowledge "appears regularly in the guise of biological determinism, threatening the fragile space for social constructionism and critical theory" (591). In other words, since the notion of gender was elaborated to argue against biological determinism and in favor of the political transformation of unequal social roles, discussing issues of "sex" seemed to lead too easily into biological determinism.

Haraway makes a point that is fundamental to her own elaboration of situated knowledges and objects as material-semiotic actors, on the one hand, and to our interest in finding in them an inspiring insight to rethink gender as a still useful historical category, on the other. She states that it was (and is) a mistake "to lose authoritative biological accounts of sex, which set up productive tensions with gender" (591): for Haraway, this leads not only to losing analytic power but also to viewing "the body itself as anything but a blank page for social inscriptions, including those of biological discourse" (591).

According to Haraway, this loss can be avoided by refusing the analytic tradition that conceives that "an object of knowledge is itself only matter for the seminal power, the act of the knower," denying to the object any kind of agency (592). This has been the case with Western notions of nature that considered it only as "the raw material of culture, appropriated, preserved, enslaved, exalted, or otherwise made flexible by disposal by culture in the logic of capitalist colonialism" (592). For Haraway, the sex-gender distinction has been designed under the assumption of this specific way of differentiating nature from culture. There is also a close relationship between the critique of the nature/culture and sex/gender distinction and the epistemological and ethical core of Haraway's framework, since situated knowledges require that the object of knowledge be pictured as an actor and agent, not as a screen, ground, or resource. Haraway adds: "The point is paradigmatically clear in critical approaches to the social and human sciences, where the agency of people studied itself transforms the entire project of producing social theory. Indeed, coming to terms with the agency of the 'objects' studied is the only way to avoid gross error and false knowledge of many kinds in these sciences" (592).

Haraway extends this claim to all sciences, not just social ones; she claims that we should consider the world neither as speaking by itself nor as disappearing in favor of us as "master decoders": "The codes of the world are not still, waiting to be read. The world is not raw material for humanization" (593). Haraway believes "the world encountered in knowledge projects is an active entity" (593). Even the body, the object of biological discourse, "becomes a most engaging being" in a way that further refuses biological determinism and any version of realism.

In sum, Haraway's redefinition of objectivity is also, in my interpretation, a contribution to the redefinition of gender as a historical category. If a key feature of Butler's performative take was their critique of the assumption that sex was a pre-discursive, ahistorical reality, with the notion of situated knowledges we grasp the historicity of our knowledge claims, in two senses: as radically contingent and as produced by a situated knowing subject. In Haraway's material-semiotic view, we found further arguments to reject biological determinism: not just because there is a history of interpretations of what the body is, but also because the body as an object of knowledge is a material-semiotic node whose boundaries (named "sex" or "gender") materialize in social interaction without being fully determined by those boundaries.[25] Moreover, if objects of knowledge are boundary projects, we can consider the narrative over the category if gender as a *history of the mapping practices of embodiment*. If such history is not determined by any founding origin nor by any final destiny, it is because bodies boundaries also shift from within.

In the following section, I will offer an overview of fields of inquiry inspired by, or/and in a critical dialogue with, gender studies and feminist theory that during the nineties and two-thousands continued the reflection on embodiment, identity, knowledge, and power.

Critical Mappings of Embodiment

Questions over embodiment that exceed the focus on gender will emerge thanks to the different inquiries that, since the nineties, intersected (more or less) polemically with feminist theory. Since it is not possible to give an exhaustive overview here, in this paragraph, I will present key insights from queer theory and trans studies, new materialism and posthumanism, decolonial feminism, and the framework of the epistemology of resistance to awaken curiosity in the reader towards these academic fields that continued remapping the body.

---

[25] Haraway is a key influence in Paul B. Preciado's historical and philosophical re-reading of feminist reflections on sex, gender, and sexuality in the twentieth-century. He claims that after World Word II there has been a change in the sex knowledge regime, from a model related to industrial-colonial capitalism (which dates back to the eighteenth century) to a second model which corresponds to postindustrial neoliberal capitalism (2018, 107–108).

Queer Theory and Trans Studies

In the nineties, new fields emerged that inquired into matters of embodiment and sexualities that cannot be reduced to gender issues: this is the case of queer theory and trans studies that pursued anti-homophobic, sexually-dissident, and anti-transphobic research and explored nonnormative sexualities, intersexuality, and transgender identity in non-pathologizing ways.

Queer theory emerged amidst the political radicalization driven by the HIV/AIDS crisis and self-critical processes within gay and lesbian communities, particularly regarding the assimilationist tendencies of dominant gay and lesbian politics (Córdoba, Sáez, and Vidarte, 2005). This radicalization questioned the integrationist tendencies of significant parts of the movement and highlighted the limits of assimilation. In the mid eighties, groups such as Act Up (AIDS Coalition to Unleash Power) and Queer Nation reclaimed the slur "queer" and transformed it into a tool for political action and resistance against normalization. This marked a shift in the subject of enunciation: "queer" was no longer an insult, but a self-designation used to signify a deliberate rupture with societal norms. The queer movement also rejected reducing gay identity to a consumable lifestyle within neoliberal society. As a post-identity movement, "queer" is not merely another identity within multicultural frameworks but a critical stance that examines the exclusion and marginalization produced by identity constructs. Thus, queer politics challenged the norms imposed by dominant heterosexual society and addressed internal processes of normalization and exclusion within gay culture, including the marginalization of lesbians, trans, and nonbinary bodies, immigrants, racialized individuals, people with disabilities, and sex workers. This critique and movement paved the way for queer politics that will influence queer theory.

Although the field of LGBT studies had been developing since the seventies, influenced by the gay liberation movement, queer theory emerged from the interest in the politics of sexuality and gender "in light of major developments in feminist theory, LGBT studies, and poststructuralism during the previous twenty years" (Turner 2004, 481). The writings by Foucault (1980), Rubin (1984), Butler (1990), and Sedgwick's *Epistemology of the Closet* (1990), were considered founding texts of queer theory.[26]

For queer theory, there is an intimate relation between normative views on gender and sexual identity and the distribution and exercise of power. Since what is considered proper or improper about sexuality has changed over time, queer theory explores "how current definitions came to be and how political action – broadly defined to include activities in social, cultural, and intellectual

---

[26] Butler and Sedgwick did not use the term "queer" in these writings, but they will use it later.

spheres – might change them" (Turner 2004, 481). However, as Rubin had already argued, Sedgwick claimed that the study of sexuality is not coextensive with the study of gender, and anti-homophobic research is not coextensive with feminist research. She also claimed that we cannot know in advance how they will differ. Sedgwick argued that the logic of concealment and revelation around the "closet" regarding LGBT identities is an interpretive key to understanding modern Western culture. Thus, LGBT identities are not only of interest to those who perceive themselves as such but to all identities since LGBT ones are used to define the entire system of cultural meanings.[27]

Teresa de Lauretis used the term "queer theory" for the first time in a lecture at the University of California in 1990 to promote a theorizing of sexuality related to a more radical politics that includes not only gay and lesbian experiences but also bisexuality, transgenderism, and intersexuality (1991).[28] For de Lauretis, "queer" is a term that rejects the politically correct connotation that she believed the formula "gay and lesbian" had acquired. Hence, queer theory is interested in "deconstructing the silences of history and in our own discursive constructions, in the differently erotic *mappings of the body, and in the imaging and enacting of new forms of communities* by the other-wise desiring subjects of this queer theory" (xvi, my emphasis).

As Turner explains, the value of the term "queer" lies in its resistance to definition: it "connotes a crossing of boundaries, the transgression of norms, and the failure to fit expected categories" (2004, 481). Queer theorists understand identity as the outcome of political (including social and cultural) processes. They share an interest in dismantling reified or substantive definitions of gender, sexuality, race, class, and other categories by "examining the particular combinations of bodies, acts, and desires that they assume in order to wonder how we might combine them differently, especially without having them become disciplinary or coercive" (482). Thus, queer theorists challenge the stability and coherence of all identity categories, appealing to previous feminist theory and LGBT studies while keeping a critical eye on those developments that rested on conservative, homophobic, or transphobic assumptions.

Trans studies are another emerging field in the nineties. Stephen Whittle claims that "trans studies is a true linking of feminist and queer theory." (2006, xii). Whittle explains that this new scholarship was informed by community activism and "started from the premise that to be trans was not to have a mental

---

[27] For an assessment of the relevance of Sedgwick's reflections to gay, lesbian, and queer history, see Bravmann (1997) and Weeks (2016). On the influential role of queer theory in LGBTI historiography, see Berger (2022, 123–124).

[28] De Lauretis (1991) claims to use the term with no reference to Queer Nation or its political actions.

or medical disorder" (xii). This premise generated a fundamental shift that enabled trans men and women "to reclaim the reality of their bodies, to create with them what they would, and to leave the linguistic determination of those bodies open to exploration and invention" (xii).

Susan Stryker (2006) claims that "transgender" in the early nineties (and "trans" more recently), became a term to refer to "a wide range of phenomena that call attention to the fact that gender, as it is lived, embodied, experienced, performed, and encountered, is more complex and varied than can be accounted for by the currently dominant binary sex/gender ideology of Eurocentric modernity" (3). It is important to highlight here that trans studies demand a critical assessment of gender not only for their theoretical framework but also for the relevance that the notion has for defending the rights of trans people:

> For the trans person's understanding of the self, the question becomes whether gender, at the heart of self-understanding, can be theoretically recuperated. It is all very well having no theoretical place within the current gendered world, but that is not the daily lived experience. Real life affords trans people constant stigma and oppression based on the apparently unreal concept of gender. This is one of the most significant issues that trans people have brought to feminist and queer theory. Homophobia and sexism are not based on your genitals or with whom you sleep, but on how you perform the self in ways that are contraindicative to the heteronormative framework (Whittle 2006, xxi).

However, there have been tensions between trans theorists and feminist work that still claims that the identity of women should be established on a biological basis, assuming by this either a natural sexual dimorphism that rules out the experience and self-perception of intersex people or a strict line of determination between the sex medically assigned at birth and gender identity, leaving transgender experiences out of the notion of womanhood.

Following Stryker, trans studies investigates embodied difference and "how such differences are transformed into social hierarchies," understood as "systems of power that operate on actual bodies, capable of producing pain and pleasure, health and sickness, punishment and reward, life and death." Stryker (2006) adds that:

> Transgender studies has a deep stake in showing how the seemingly anomalous, minor, exotic, or strange qualities of transgender phenomena are in fact effects of the relationship constructed between those phenomena and sets of norms that are themselves culturally produced and enforced. Transgender studies enables a critique of the conditions that cause transgender phenomena to stand out in the first place, and that allow gender normativity to disappear into the unanalyzed, ambient background. Ultimately, it is not just

transgender phenomena per se that are of interest, but rather the manner in which these phenomena reveal the operations of systems and institutions that simultaneously produce various possibilities of viable personhood, and eliminate others (3)

Stryker's words point toward another bias in normative notions of sex and gender and previous feminist reflections: cisexism. Julia Serano (2007) defines it as the belief that the self-perceived gender of trans people is inferior or less authentic than that of cis people. The categories of "cis" and "trans" have today become part of popular speech, although this does not mean that there is social acceptance of this distinction. "Cis-gender" is used to refer to people who feel in conformity with the gender they were assigned at birth according to the medical definition of their genitalia. The critique of this bias as part of what we could now call the *cis*-heterosexual matrix makes the dialogue between feminist theory and trans studies fundamental: "far from being an inconsequentially narrow specialization dealing *only* with a rarified population of transgender individuals, or with an eclectic collection of esoteric transgender practices, [trans studies] represents a significant and ongoing critical engagement with some of the most trenchant issues in contemporary humanities, social science, and biomedical research" (Stryker 2006, 3–4).[29]

To conclude this section, it is interesting to mention a recent publication in the journal *Nature* by science journalist Claire Ainsworth (2015) entitled "Sex Redefined." In this piece, Ainsworth reviews contemporary developments that show that the idea of two sexes is simplistic and that biologists are thinking that there is a broader spectrum than that. Ainsworth concludes that "if biologists continue to show that sex is a spectrum, then society and state will have to grapple with the consequences, and work out where and how to draw the line" (291). Hence, there are promising alliances between biomedical science mapping the sex spectrum and feminist, queer, and trans studies.

New Materialism and Posthumanism

New materialism refers to a series of reflections developed in the two-thousands which claim that there has been an excessive focus on discourse, language, and power in previous "hegemonic" constructivist and poststructuralist inquiries and that it has come the moment to return instead to insufficiently explored questions of materiality, biology, and the current knowledge offered by the life and natural sciences. Although this is one common central tenet, new materialisms encompass diverse frameworks and positions.

---

[29] Stryker's *Transgender History* (2008) is a paradigmatic example of the application of a trans studies' perspective to historical writing.

The same can be said about posthumanism. Rosi Braidotti defines posthuman critical theory as unfolding at the intersection between posthumanism and postanthropocentrism: "The former proposes the philosophical critique of the Western Humanist ideal of 'Man' as the allegedly universal measure of all things, whereas the latter rests on the rejection of species hierarchy and human exceptionalism" (2018, 339).[30] Braidotti also claims that there is a particular relevance of posthuman critical theory in the face of the current Anthropocene condition: "an environmental, social-economical, as well as affective and psychical phenomenon of unprecedented proportions. The combination of fast technological advances on the one hand and growing economic and social inequalities on the other makes for a conflict-ridden landscape marked by violent and inhumane power relations." (339).

Ewa Domańska (2019, 2021) has shown that these reflections impacted historiography:

> A growing interest in post-anthropocentric (and/or posthumanist) approaches to animal history, biohistory, environmental history, history of things, the emergence of new subfields such as big history and neurohistory as well as discussions about the Anthropocene and climate change, non-human agency, relations between humans and non-humans, the question of scale and non-anthropocentric conceptions of time (geological time) are all signs of post-humanist marks on the discipline of history (2019, 328).

Moreover, for Domańska, the new questions posed by posthumanism and new materialism led to an ongoing shift from an interpretivist-constructivist paradigm to a posthumanist and/or ecological one in the humanities and social sciences at large (2021, 186). Gender studies and queer theory, as well as the narrativist moment in theory of history, belong, according to Domańska, to the previous paradigm. Hence, she considers that these fields are moving "from textualism to (new) materialism" (189).

This Element has shown that feminist research on sex and gender demands us to redefine how we understand "humanity." In relation to history, Domańska believes that posthumanism also contributes to this task since "It challenges the very foundations of history understood as a specific approach to the past developed within the framework of Greco-Roman and Judeo-Christian traditions with their anthropocentric (and even zoocentric) bias, Eurocentrism, geocentrism, and even exclusive human authorship of knowledge building" (2019, 337). However, Domańska claims that posthumanist history as a subfield of historical reflection does not exist as such. For Domańska, its primary

---

[30] Haraway's cyborg manifesto (1991, 149–181) is a common reference for posthumanist reflections. For a fuller understanding of Braidotti's view, see Braidotti (2013).

influence has been in environmental and animal history, where the insights offered by Hawaray, Braidotti, and Karen Barad have been crucial in motivating this paradigm shift.[31] Hence, the writings of these thinkers have promoted new questions and modes of research that extend beyond feminist debates.

Stefan Berger (2022) also acknowledges the impact of new materialism in his thorough review of the development of gender history. Referring to the "material turn" in feminist theory, Berger highlights the relevance of Barad's founding piece "Posthumanist Performativity: Toward an Understanding of How Matter Comes to Matter" (2003), along with Stacy Alaimo's and Susan Hekman's 2008 edited volume *Material Feminisms* (256).[32] A critical engagement with these perspectives requires a thorough analysis of the similarities and differences between the various understandings of materiality and the posthuman that have been developed since the two-thousands. Depending on the author, materiality sometimes refers to nature, biology, and/or the environment, while others associate it with material objects as "things." In the words of Alaimo and Hekman (2008), Barad – along with Haraway – "have developed theories that define the human, nonhuman, technological, and natural as agents that jointly construct the parameters of our common world" (5). Given its status as a founding text, I will briefly present Barad's agential realism to provide a general idea of the theoretical challenges posed by posthumanism and new materialism to feminist theory.

Barad establishes a critical dialogue with performativity theory since they claim that there are humanist assumptions in Butler's work that should be abandoned.[33] Thus, Barad wants to extend Butler's theory beyond the realm of the human and into matter itself to offer a posthumanist performative metaphysics.[34] As Mariela Solana explains, for Barad, "the subject of performativity is not the human being but the universe itself; it is the world that acts generating all sorts of entities that did not exist previously to the immanent differentiating processes" (2024, 210–211).[35]

Building on feminist, queer, and science studies, in general, and especially from Haraway's redefinition of objects of knowledge as material-semiotic

---

[31] For an overview on animal history and Haraway's influence in it, see Fudge (2019). Barad's influence can also be trace in the history of emotions and sport history. See Barclay (2017) and Thorpe, H., Brice, J. and Clark, M. (2021). I thank Ewa Domańska for this information and for generously sharing with me her expertise on these new trends in historical writing.

[32] For critical assessments on feminist new materialism see Ahmed (2008), Solana (2024), and La Greca and Solana (2024).

[33] I will be referring to Barad with they/them pronouns as they prefer.

[34] Butler's original presentation of the theory of gender performativity was an anti-metaphysical view since it consisted of a genealogical critique of the discourse on gender in feminist theory.

[35] However, Haraway has clarified that her position should be considered a critique of human exceptionalism, rather than a posthumanist view. I thank Julieta Massacese for this information.

actors, Barad pursues the task of rethinking the relationship between discursive practices and material phenomena in a posthumanist way. To that aim, they claim that the notion of discursivity "cannot be founded on an inherent distinction between humans and nonhumans" (2003, 818):

> Discursive practices are often confused with linguistic expression, and meaning is often thought to be a property of words. Hence, discursive practices and meanings are said to be peculiarly human phenomena. But, if this is true, how would it be possible to take account of the boundary-making practices by which the differential constitution of "humans" and "nonhumans" are enacted? (818)

Barad also follows Foucault's notion of discourse (as "not what is said" but "that which constrains and enables what can be said") and defines discursive practices as the "actual historically situated social conditions" that produce, rather than describe, the subjects and objects of knowledge practices (819). With poststructuralism, we came to understand that discursive practices are situated and historical. Barad argues that this is also true of matter.

Barad builds her position upon the critique of the nature/culture dualism offered by Butler and Haraway and rejects the characterization of matter as just a blank surface "passively awaiting signification." Barad adds: "Matter is not support, location, referent, or source of sustainability for discourse" nor does it require "the mark of an external force like culture or history to complete it" (821). Thus, Barad combines the idea that discursive practices are not merely human phenomena with a view of matter as active, dynamic, and integral to the process of meaning making to propose an "agentic realism"[36]: "In an agential realist account, matter does not refer to a fixed substance; rather, matter is substance in its intra-active becoming – not a thing, but a doing, a congealing of agency. Matter is a stabilizing and destabilizing process of iterative intra-activity." (822)[37]

The last quote illustrates Barad's expansion of the notion of performativity in a posthumanist direction, as what is said of matter is what Butler claimed about gender, but now with the metaphysical addition of making "the world" the "subject" of the process. In Barad's agential realism, discursive practices and materiality coemerge, and this co-emergence is called "intra-action." Thus, Barad stresses that both elements in the relation are agentic and that they do not "inter-act": they do not exist as such before their relation; they "intra-act."

---

[36] Karen Barad develops her version of feminist new materialism through attention to physics, specifically Niels Bohr Bohr's account of scientific apparatuses (Barad 2003, 818).
[37] Haraway, however, refrained from considering her own position a realist one.

Moreover, for Barad, matter is not immutable: it is "an ongoing historicity" (821).

As I mentioned before, for Barad, agential realism would avoid holding the category of "humanity" fixed – a critical insight already developed by feminist theorists, as we have seen, but now connected to an insistence on reconsidering this notion from a perspective that rejects human exceptionalism and traces the intimate relation of our discursive practices with the nonhuman (whether it is considered as matter, nature, or biology). Barad believes that their view also avoids the dichotomy between strict determinism and unconstrained freedom, insofar as they claim that intra-actions are constraining but not determining, making the future radically open (826). For Barad, possibilities of acting "exist at every moment" and, with them, the "responsibility to intervene in the world's becoming, to contest and rework what matters and what is excluded from mattering" (827).[38]

In her review of the impact of posthumanist and new materialist reflections on historical writing, Domańska does not mention examples of posthumanist gender historiography. Nevertheless, she stresses the connection between gender theory and posthumanism insofar as they both seek to critically reconsider the limits and exclusions of the humanist definition of the human being (2019, 336). For Domańska, redefining the relations between the human and nonhuman should enable a critical view on the affirmation of humanity and a historiography attuned to its time as well as future-oriented (332). It is also important to note that, although Domańska argues about the relevance of these new frameworks for historical studies, in a recent publication with Zoltan Boldizár Simon and Marek Tamm she has also debated the "promises and pitfalls" of anthropocenic historical knowledge (Simon, Tamm, and Domańska 2021).

Berger does register the impact of feminist new materialism in the writing of gender historians who are working within the broader framework of the history of material culture. He considers that in this historiographical practice, gender historians "have also massively advanced our decoding of the construction of gendered identities" (2022, 256). Berger refers to histories of material objects or "things" (like spatial arrangements in pubs or clothing) that trace how "Gender informs things and, in turn, the things that people own inform conceptions and

---

[38] Mariela Solana (2024) has written on the theoretical opportunities that new feminist materialisms find in an alliance with the life and natural sciences for feminist reflections. However, Solana warns us that this should not result in a re-inscription of the old hierarchy between the (superior) natural and (inferior) social sciences and humanities, but in a horizontal, creative exchange. Simon makes a similar argument in relation to current historiography in Simon, Z. B., Tamm, M., & Domańska, E. (2021, 415–419).

perceptions of gender in wide-ranging ways" (Greig, Hamlet, and Hannan quoted in Berger 2022, 256).

Regardless of the virtues and problems these ongoing inquiries may have, their contribution to the intersection between debates over gender and theory of history could lie in their further development of two key insights from previous feminist work: on the one hand, the need to reconsider how we define "humanity" after a critical reflection over the exclusions such definition can imply and/or reproduce, and, on the other, the theoretical and ethical gains that approaching our objects of study in terms of relationality instead of dichotomy may offer.[39] Following Domańska and Berger, we may draw inspiration for alternative ways of approaching the past in dialogue with post-humanist and new materialist research. Attention to materiality, biology, and nature as dynamic and fully historical phenomena can offer new insights into our understanding of sex and gender. However, I believe that such dialogue should not lose sight of a feminist hallmark: the vigilant critique of any form of biological determinism or exclusionary definition of embodiment.[40]

Decolonial Feminism and the Epistemology of Resistance

The critique of humanism and "the subject" that was part of poststructuralist debates also constitutes an important backdrop to the rise of the post-imperial and interdisciplinary terrain in which postcolonial and decolonial theory arose.[41] If in Barad's perspective the posthuman return to materiality rejects any fixed definition of the distinction between human and nonhuman, and opened the way to inquiries into nonhuman realities (such as atoms and bacteria), in post-imperialist perspectives the focus has been on those people and cultures who were colonized and denied the dignity of humanity. In a similar vein to black feminism and intersectionality studies, the history and effects of colonization show the need for feminist theory to revise theorizations of gender in its close and complicated relation with issues of race and imperial power.

María Lugones's 2008 essay, "The Coloniality of Power," offers insights into the relationship between gender, race, and colonization, as well as the continuing effects of imperialism. It reintroduces the issue of race through a reflection on colonial rule as a historically specific way – whose effects are still present – in which the fixed boundaries of "the human" have excluded some subjects by

---

[39] Moulton (2023) draws from Barad's concept of intra-action to develop a non-binary historical methodology for gender history in a close dialogue with queer theory and trans studies.

[40] For a detailed discussion on the virtues and limits of new feminist materialist theorizations of embodiment, see Gayle Salomon's critique of Elizabeth Grozs' claims on materiality and sexual difference in Salomon (2010, 145–168).

[41] For an introduction to postcolonialism within theory of history see Majumdar (2022).

imposing on their precolonial communities frames of gender that were not part of their social relations. Lugones's view allows us to see at work the critical insights developed by Third World and Women of Color feminists and critical race theorists, emphasizing intersectionality. At the same time, she uses the criticism of the eighties definition of gender to stress its Western-modern specificity.

Lugones elaborates the concept of "modern/colonial gender system" by putting together a feminist and intersectional framework with Anibal Quijano's view on the "coloniality of power."[42] Quijano considers global, Eurocentered capitalist power as organized around two axes he names "the coloniality of power" and "modernity." As Lugones explains: "Both 'race' and gender find their meanings in this model [*patrón*]. Quijano understands that all power is structured in relations of domination, exploitation and conflict as social actors fight over control of 'the four basic areas of human existence: sex, labor, collective authority and subjectivity/intersubjectivity, their resources and products'" (Quijano quoted in Lugones, 2008, 2).

In Quijano's model, the invention of "race" as the basic and universal social classification of the population of the planet was "a pivotal turn as it replaces the relations of superiority and inferiority established through domination. It reconceives humanity and human relations fictionally, in biological terms" (Lugones, 2008, 2). This classification was not only central to global capitalism but also for "the historical disputes over control of labor, sex, collective authority and inter-subjectivity as developing in processes of long duration, rather than understanding each of the elements as pre-existing the relations of power" (3). In this respect, Lugones highlights that in Quijano's view the elements that constitute the global, Eurocentered, capitalist model of power "do not stand in separation from each other and none of them is prior to the processes that constitute the patterns. Indeed, the mythical presentation of these elements as metaphysically prior is an important aspect of the cognitive model of Eurocentered, global capitalism" (3).

The coloniality of power establishes relations of superiority and inferiority in a way that conceives "humanity" as a hierarchical difference determined in biological terms. Biological determinism, again, justifies the reproduction of unequal power relations: "In constituting this social classification, coloniality permeates all aspects of social existence and gives rise to new social and geocultural identities (Quijano, 2000b, 342). 'America' and 'Europe' are among the new geocultural identities. 'European,' 'Indian,' 'African' are

---

[42] Joao Ohara (2022) has reflected on the decolonial turn in Latin America in his excellent overview of the current theory and philosophy of history and its "global variations."

among the 'racial' identities." Lugones adds: "With the expansion of European colonialism, the classification was imposed on the population of the planet. Since then, it has permeated every area of social existence and it constitutes the most effective form of material and inter-subjective social domination." (Lugones, 2008, 3)

However, Lugones points out that Quijano's framework uncritically assumed the specific modern Eurocentric notion of gender and the patriarchal, heterosexual, and sexual dimorphic understanding. In this regard, Quijano's view continues to "veil the ways in which non-'white' colonized women were subjected and disempowered" (2). Since Quijano understands sex as biological attributes that become elaborated as social categories, he accepts the opposition between sex and gender that has already been criticized. By putting Quijano's framework in dialogue with an intersectional framework and the work by Third World and Women of Color feminists and critical race theorists, Lugones shows that the Western definition of gender was part of the cultural imposition to precolonial societies that either had different gender arrangements or no gender system was in place at all.

For example, the research by Oyèrónkẹ́ Oyěwùmí showed that "gender was not an organizing principle in Yoruba society prior to colonization by the West" (Oyěwùmí quoted in Lugones 2008, 8). Their social categories were neither binarily opposed nor hierarchical, and sexual dimorphism was not a feature of gender arrangements either. Hence, "For females, colonization was a twofold process of racial inferiorization and gender subordination. The creation of 'women' as a category was one of the very first accomplishments of the colonial state" (Oyěwùmí quoted in Lugones 2008, 8).

It is for this reason that Lugones proposes the notion of the *modern/colonial gender system* to fully understand the extent to which the imposition of this gender system was as constitutive of the coloniality of power as the coloniality of power was constitutive of it. The colonial/modern gender system "could not exist without the coloniality of power, given that the classification of the population in terms of race is a necessary condition of its possibility" (Lugones 2008, 12).

Lugones describes the modern/colonial gender system as having a "light" and a "dark" side. The first one orders the lives of white bourgeois men and women, and it constitutes the modern/colonial meaning of "men" and "women": it is a patriarchal, heterosexual, and binary system by which white bourgeois females are defined by sexual purity and passivity, they are ban from the sphere of collective authority, from the production of knowledge, from most of control over the means of production. Lugones believes that Eurocentered global capitalism only recognizes sexual dimorphism for white bourgeois males and females.

The "dark" side "was and is thoroughly violent": those understood as "non-white women" were not only excluded from decision-making, economics, and rituals but also reduced to animality, "to forced sex with white colonizers, to such deep labor exploitation that often people died working" (16). Also, they were not necessarily understood dimorphically: "Sexual fears of colonizers led them to imagine the indigenous people of the Americas as hermaphrodites or intersexed, with large penises and breasts with flowing milk. However, as Gunn Allen and others make clear, intersexed individuals were recognized in many tribal societies prior to colonization without assimilation to the sexual binary" (7).

For these reasons, Lugones considers that to understand how colonialism and global Eurocentered capitalism organized sex and gender, it is crucial to understand the changes that colonization brought. If the naturalization of sexual differences is another product of the modern use of science (as Quijano claimed regarding "race"), Lugones concludes: "as with other assumption characteristics it is important to ask how sexual dimorphism served and serves Eurocentered global capitalist domination/exploitation" (7).

At the beginning of this piece, Lugones claimed that she aimed to unveil the reach and consequences of complicity with the colonial/modern gender system that subjects women and men of color "in all domains of existence" in order to "place ourselves in a position to call each other to reject this gender system as we perform a transformation of communal relations" (1). Moreover, she adds that her interest in the intersection of race, class, gender, and sexuality lies in understanding "the indifference that men, but, more importantly to our struggles, men who have been racialized as inferior, exhibit to the systematic violences inflicted upon women of color" (1). Lugones wants to understand the construction of this indifference that she believes is not just an epistemological question related to "not seeing the violence" because of the categorial separation of race, gender, class, and sexuality.

The issue of indifference to oppression, both epistemologically and politically, has been a persistent concern of liberatory projects. Although Lugones rightly points out that it is not just a matter of knowledge – as if a better epistemological framework could solve it – this does not mean that it is not *also* an epistemological issue. Lugones's essay is an example of the effort to theorize subjectivity in its historical, situated forms, which involves comprehending this kind of indifference as well. In another article, Lugones defines his project as *decolonial feminism*, as it pursues the possibility of overcoming the coloniality of gender (2010, 747).

A recent development in feminist philosophy and critical race theory addresses this last challenge directly: I am referring to José Medina's

Epistemology of Resistance (2013). I will conclude this section with Medina's work as it enables this Element to reconnect the refiguration of the category of gender with its epistemic and political relevance in current public debates related to women's and LGBTIQ+ human rights worldwide.

Medina takes part in the debates over epistemologies of injustices to explore the epistemic side of oppression and resistance and argues for a polyphonic contextualism combining developments in feminist, queer, and critical race theory.[43] Medina is interested in investigating how gender and sexual ignorance, racial ignorance, and their interrelations "are produced by systems of oppression, what their ramifications in our social and personal lives are, and what we can do to resist them" (14).

Following Foucault, Medina claims that "resistance is a complicated and heterogeneous phenomenon that defies unification and explication according to abstract and rigid principles of subversion." Moreover, he adds: "Our cognitive, affective and political lives are permeated by different forms of conformity and resistance that shape our lives in various (and not always coherent) ways" (14). Hence, we are shaped by systems of oppression but also by the various forms of resistance that emerge within and around them.

Medina reflects on the epistemic aspects of our social interactions "that take place in complex and diverse communities under conditions of oppression and on the *resistance* that we can find in those interactions" (3). Epistemic injustices, Medina explains, are pervasive not only in nondemocratic societies but also in democratic ones.[44] Hence, they call for epistemic resistance as "the use of our epistemic resources and abilities to undermine and change oppressive normative structures and the complacent cognitive-affective functioning that sustains those structures" (3).

If resistance can be exerted from multiple social locations and differently positioned subjects relate to power in different ways, then understanding its diverse and heterogeneous forms requires understanding as well "the positionality and relationality of social agents in networks of power relations" (15). This has been precisely what my alternative narrative on gender highlighted as the critical gain from debates since the seventies. Moreover, Medina recalls that for Foucault, resistance is never in a position of exteriority in relation to power since power has a relational character. This means, for Medina, that resistance

---

[43] Although this Element focuses on the debates over the category of gender, we have already seen (thanks to black feminism, intersectional studies and decolonial feminism) that issues of class and race are also relevant in any specific research on gender. By incorporating Medina's framework, I aim to inform the reader about a current line of research that examines our epistemic and social practices taking into account both issues of gender and race.

[44] For examples of epistemic injustices see Medina (2013, 3).

can be exerted both within and around our discursive practices, at the center as well as at their periphery.[45] Hence, Medina's contextualist account covers cases of internal resistance as well as cases of external resistance "for the multifaceted activity of *resisting* is conceptualized as *contending with,* and not exclusively or fundamentally as *contending against*" (16). Since there lies a key insight for the conclusion of this Element, I quote Medina at large:

> Experiences and practices of resistance should not be understood exclusively, or even primarily, in oppositional terms, as if resisting were always a matter of opposing from the outside, of experiencing a clash of wholly distinct opposing forces. Resistance often takes other phenomenological shapes. It can feel more like being pulled in different directions from the inside, *like being torn from within*. Experiencing resistance can often be like feeling a rupture that one does not know what to do with (at least initially), like feeling perplexity (16, my emphasis).

As Medina explains, there is an intimate connection between our sensibilities and our cognitive potential. In the foreword to his book, he claims – similarly to Lugones – that its key theme is insensitivity: "being cognitively and affectively numbed to the lives of others: being inattentive to and unconcerned by their experiences, problems, and aspiration; and being unable to connect with them and to understand their speech and action" (xi). Medina believes this kind of insensitivity is at the core of epistemic injustices. That is also why he argues that "racial and sexual insensibilities result as much in lack of knowledge of social realities as in lack of self-knowledge (or knowledge of one's own positionality and relationality with respect to the relevant categories and the relevant forms of oppression)" (18).[46]

Although there would be much more to say to present Medina's take on the epistemology of resistance adequately, I would like to mention that he considers the women's movement as a paradigmatic example of the resistance to a large-scale system of oppression that we find "in the most familiar and intimate aspects of our epistemic life, within ourselves and our sensibilities" (18). Medina recalls that the numerous voices in the women's movement had resisted "deficient social sensibilities and their blind spots, triggering *a process of social learning* that benefits us all, for their activism expanded our sensibilities and taught us to pay attention to the interrelations between public practices and our most intimate feelings, emotions, desires, and beliefs." (18, my emphasis). It is

---

[45] Medina adds that epistemology should also attend to the varieties of resistance – more or less planned and intentional, even unconscious – in daily lives, as in every discursive practice and location.

[46] Medina exemplifies this with Charles Mill's notion of *white ignorance,* which resounds with Ware's position, as we saw.

also worth mentioning that, for Medina, democratic social interaction requires resistance.

Finally, Medina highlights that resistance "begins *at home*, in the most intimate aspects of our cognitive-affective functioning (...) within ourselves and in the activities in which we feel at home" (18). This implies putting our perspective in communicative interaction with the perspective of others, to become exposed to challenges, to processes of self-questioning or *self-estrangement,* "that is, processes of deep self-interrogation in which we become strangers to ourselves." Medina claims that, by becoming perplexed about who we are, we can look at ourselves with fresh eyes. I agree with Medina's conclusion that we have learned this from feminist, queer, and critical race theory: "the importance of unmasking and undoing *the process of social construction of our perspective*, of interrupting the flow of familiarity and obviousness, making the familiar unfamiliar and the obvious bizarre" (19, my emphasis). The previous trajectory of debates can be considered exactly as that: as a process of unmasking and undoing the social construction of our sex-gender perspective.

My reading of the debates over the usefulness of the category of gender, the limits of its original understanding as a social construction, along with the critical contribution of poststructuralist reflections, performativity, and the semiotic-material nature of embodiment leads to the conclusion that we have today a richer idea of the relation between bodies, knowledge, and power. The severe self-criticism that feminist theorists developed regarding their fundamental category amounts to a more promising framework for grasping the complexity of embodiment as a historical, theoretical, and political process. Following Medina, we can claim that the debates that this Element has reviewed allowed the different perspectives involved to engage in a communicative interaction, challenging the way that gender has been understood and provoking a process of self-interrogation within feminist theory that has even fostered the creation of new academic fields that further expanded the research on identity, embodiment, knowledge, and power.

These diverse mappings of embodiment may bring to mind Foucault's famous antihumanist claim in "Nietzsche, Genealogy, History": that "Nothing in man – not even his body – is sufficiently stable to serve as the basis of self-recognition or for understanding other men" (Foucault 1984, 87–88). Scott echoed this phrase in the introduction to his classic 1988 book to reflect on feminist research. She wrote: "Nothing about the body, including women's reproductive organs, determines universally how social difference will be shaped" (1999, 2). After this journey through feminist debates, we can accept the conclusion that nothing is sufficiently stable – neither categories of identities nor the body itself. However, we also arrive at another realization: that the historicity of knowledge claims and power arrangements points toward the *instability of embodiment* as a basis for understanding others. It would not be a metaphysical or epistemological basis, but it can be an ethical one: a realization that informs our critical positioning as subjects of knowledge and promotes inquiries that explore and affirm human complexity (Butler 2019).

In Section 4, I will elaborate on the usefulness of the refigured category of gender for historians and theorists of history interested in bringing a more complex understanding of embodiment to their practice.

4 Gender, Past and Present of the Theory of History: A Relational View of Embodiment

In this final section, I will present three conclusions that can be drawn from the previous reflection on gender, which amount to a useful framework for historians and theorists of history, as well as for anyone interested in fostering an informed perspective on the relationship between bodies, knowledge, and politics. First, the interpretation I presented of the trajectory of feminist debates as the refiguration of gender as a historical category offers a series of insights that we can define as *a relational view of embodiment*.[47] Second, this view retains the critical perspective on gender as a social construction in a sophisticated way since it avoids dualistic assumptions on the relation between nature and culture, and sex and gender at the same time that it rejects biological determinism. Third, the reflection on gender offers an opportunity to reread the narrative on the past and present of the theory of history and to link it to the current context of public debates.

The main insight that we gain from this Element is an awareness of how categories of identity and embodiment relate to each other. Rather than considering categories of identity as concepts that have a fixed reference, they should be understood as ways of organizing bodily boundaries in both an epistemic and political sense. The refigured notion of gender leads to a relational view of embodiment insofar as it enables an understanding of the diverse features of *embodied* subjectivity. The body emerges within a network of overlapping (sometimes opposing or even contradictory) relations due to boundary-constituting as well as boundary-shifting practices. Boundary-constituting practices may include the theoretical, scientific, and artistic projects that take the body as its object of study, the policies and legislation that establish normative

---

[47] In La Greca (2024), I elaborated on a relational ontology of the body that complements the conclusions of this Element.

definitions of "sex," "gender," and "sexuality," the social norms (formal and informal, explicit and implicit ones) that regulate the "proper way" of behaving and appearing in public, and the reward or punishment they entail for the adjustment to, or deviation from them. Boundary-shifting practices refer to those that figure the body as a material-semiotic actor, rather than a passive surface or entity. Among the possibilities of boundary-shifting, we can include resistance and social activism: sex, gender, and sexuality boundaries have shifted over time when social movements, like the women and LGBTQI+ ones, happened. That is why, following Medina, we can relate boundary-shifting practices to both external and internal forms of resistance that have political and epistemic effects. How this happens is a contextual issue: as Scott claimed in relation to the elements of her definition of gender, how these practices unfold in a specific time and place is a historical question.[48]

Since identities and bodies are both situated phenomena, historical research is fundamental to tracing the different ways that categories of identity and embodiment have been understood and socially organized in the past, and it can also contribute to exploring how these categories continue to be reproduced in more recent political and ideological conflicts and as the current context clearly demands. A relational approach, then, enables us to frame the relationship between embodiment and categories of identity as an open-ended, historical dynamic.

Although there is no need to adopt a radical social constructivist view to argue against biological determinism, historical research should proceed without ahistorical assumptions regarding sex, gender, and sexuality. As we have seen, the critical insight that constructionism, poststructuralism, and/or the linguistic turn have offered is that categories of identity emerge in specific time and place contexts and are subject to change. Hence, they are provisional. As we have seen, the constructivist one-directional understanding of the relationship between nature and culture, discourse, and materiality, made it impossible to grasp the generative possibilities of meaning and bodies in their interaction with the boundaries within which they emerge. Butler and

---

[48] Deciding which practices may constitute or shift boundaries deserves a contextual analysis since a change in legislation, for example, could produce a shifting of boundaries, and not just the constitution of them. For example, this could be the case of gender identity legislation that acknowledges the rights of trans, intersex, nonbinary and gender-non-conforming people to live and be recognized in public in the way they self-perceive their gender identity (when, historically, these subjects had been forced to comply with ideal norms of sex and gender that had no room for their embodied experiences). However, a successful shift in boundaries may turn into a constitution of new ones. Hence, this should be considered as a contextual issue and evolving distinction. Of course, if the changes in boundaries will have emancipatory or oppressive effects, we cannot know in advance. Therefore, historical research is fundamental to trace these practices.

Haraway contributed to the historical refiguration of the category of gender by understanding embodied subjectivity in a more complex perspective than a mere constructivist interpretation: they both rejected the view of gender as an imposed cultural interpretation to pre-discursive sex that reduced the body to a passive blank page for active social inscriptions.

The critical dialogue between feminist, queer, trans and, intersectional studies, and activism leads to acknowledging that categories of identity have historically produced the exclusion of some subjects from conventional historical narratives, from fully participating in democratic life, and even from the very definition (and, hence, dignity) of humanity. Keeping this ethical insight in mind, a relational view highlights that categories of identity constitute the boundaries of bodies but do not determine them: the body is not an inert entity. Embodiment is a relational phenomenon. Although it is partially produced by the categories that are used to define, study or control it, embodiment is not a mere effect of our mapping practices: its boundaries can shift from within. In other words, notions such as "woman," "men," and "human" have historical meanings produced in social-power relations, but those meanings and relations shift in their interaction.[49] The contingency of embodiment explains the intimate relation between knowledge and politics that makes categories of identity at the same time generative of meaning and bodies, and always open to their own remaking. Contexts of activism, academic, and public debate as the current one, are privileged moments for witnessing the relational nature of embodiment as its boundaries and categories are contested, redefined, and renegotiated.

Thus, the usefulness of a refigured notion of gender for theory and history should not be of interest solely to those engaging in some form of feminist research – as Scott already claimed four decades ago. Its interest neither lies in any specific definition of the notion but rather in *how thinking about gender works*: its relational insight. The current global scenario of debates over gender presents theorists of history – both those already working in this diverse and dynamic field, and those eager to join it – with a historical experience of a moment where the terms of humanity and embodiment are being overtly contested and negotiated again. The theoretical and empirical body of work accumulated over the past five decades provides both academics and activists resources to identify how those boundaries shifted in the past and to imagine how they can be negotiated now in a process that will demand us to rewrite historical narratives once again.

---

[49] Barad claims that the idea of "interaction" leads us to believe in the prior existence of the elements that inter-act, while her notion of intra-action implies that the "elements" or "relata" do not have a previous existence. I hesitate to fully subscribe to Barad's notion of intra-action, but I consider their observation on the term "interaction" insightful.

We need categories of identity to understand human life in its diverse forms, but we also know that they are not neutral notions. They are produced within webs of power relations; hence, they describe as much as they constitute *human* life (even the notion of "human" and its other, the "nonhuman"). Since categories of identity are part of our basic vocabulary, it is crucial to understand that the same words do not have the same meanings in every context, as meaning is generated in specific knowledge-power arrangements and in the interrelationship with other categories. Moreover, issues of identity are not just a matter of definitions; they are also a question of uses and effects, of political struggle and its consequences.

The relational view of embodiment retains the critical insight that gender is a social construction, a hallmark of its definition in the eighties, but it no longer assumes a dichotomic understanding of nature versus culture. The reflections presented in this Element demonstrate that feminist theory does not reject biology per se, but rather its deterministic understanding or uses, and their political consequences: what is rejected is the assumption that natural differences explain and justify social and political ones. In a relational view, then, nature and culture are both historical realities. Hence, historians and theorists of history can not only benefit from applying this view in their research, but they can also contribute to developing it by reflecting on the way that our understanding of history has changed to encompass not only human culture but nature, biology, and the nonhuman world.

As the refigured notion of gender, the relational view of embodiment follows the spirit of Haraway's situated knowledges by avoiding the dichotomic trap of objectivity (as value neutrality) versus relativism while acknowledging the positionality of the subject of knowledge. The issues of constructivism, relativism, and the responsibility of the historian's writing have been part of the recent past of philosophy and theory of history. The critical interventions by Hayden White (1973) and others produced a highly polemical and productive moment usually referred to as the linguistic or narrativist turn since the late seventies (see Ankersmit and Kellner 1995). The claim that the way that we talk about the past not merely describes but also constitutes it was one of its central tenets: discussions abounded over how historical discourse "constructs" the past as an object of study, to what extent and what, then, are the epistemic and political consequences. Scott (1991) herself had a protagonist role with her critique of conventional history as a foundational practice that contributed to the exclusion of marginalized subjects (such as women, gay, lesbian, black or indigenous people) from its grand narratives.

At the beginning of the two-thousands, a tragic narrative also appeared within the philosophy of history regarding what some theorists considered the "exhausted textualist dead-end" to which narrativist debates had driven historical theory and they presented different arguments and topics to shift the focus of the field leaving questions of language or discourse behind (Ankermist 2005; Runia 2006). However, even among theorists interested in moving discussions forward and exploring new topics, this narrative of total discontinuity with the past is not universally accepted (see Partner 2009; La Greca 2014; Kleinberg 2017; Pihlainen 2017; Tozzi Thompson 2022). For that reason, this Element argues that we can reread the trajectory of debates within theory of history taking inspiration from the case of gender and feminist theory. Moreover, Berger's *History and Identity. How Historical Theory shapes Historical Practice* (2022) has recently offered a thorough and detailed reconstruction of how theory of history has impacted the practice and writings of historians since the seventies. Berger focuses on the intimate relationship between historiography and identity and refers to the influence of constructivist, narrativist, and poststructuralist theories to argue that historians have become more self-reflexive about their practice and, particularly, to their own positionality.[50]

As was the case with the tragic narrative on gender in feminist theory, the narrativist past can be reread, borrowing from Medina's framework, as amounting to a similar process of social learning since those debates highlighted the positionality of the subject of knowledge and the role of historical discourse not just in our knowledge of the past but also in our understanding of the present.[51] In other words, historical writing has also contributed to constituting the boundaries of the body insofar as it has offered perspectives on how "humanity" has been defined, who has been considered "more" or "less" human, and which subjects have thus been excluded, marginalized or left out of history. Historical discourse has been – and it still is today – a boundary practice, sometimes constituting, sometimes shifting our comprehension of embodiment.

Following Medina, since resistance "begins at home," we could say that the strong theoretical debates that the linguistic turn provoked within theory of history have produced a sense of perplexity regarding the historical profession self-image but, as Berger claims, they also allowed historians to acknowledge their positionality as an integral part of their epistemic practice. Against any emplotment that would consider the past of theory of history over and done with, we can find an epistemic promise in this (disciplinary) process of *being torn from within*: an expansion of our social sensibilities. Thus, what lies ahead are research paths that will not be numbed to the lives of others and will foster

---

[50] For an interpretation of White's and Scott's theoretical work as implying a re-narration of historiography as an academic discipline, see La Greca (2016).

[51] For a thorough exploration of the concept of the "present" in the context of history, see Mudrovcic (2024).

resistance to previous insensitivities that have been unveiled thanks to the impact of liberatory social movements.

Sex-gender activism broke social silences, challenged social assumptions, and disrupted public space to claim for better living conditions for *every*-body. Thus, it highlighted that academic responsibilities are also democratic ones. A theory of history that acknowledges the impossibility of disentangling knowledge and power does not fall into relativism, on the contrary, it finds the ethical ground for historical writing.

Since we are witnessing another moment of "furor" around gender, the trajectory of this category has not ended. The present context is another ongoing episode of the contested production of gender meanings where theoretical reflection can foster power-sensitive conversations. Thus, this Element aims to provide the reader with an updated map of reflections on sex, gender, and embodiment not just as an introduction to the debates of the last five decades but also as an invitation to contribute to the ethical demands of the theory and practice of history for our times.

References

Ahmed, S. (2008). Some Preliminary Remarks on the Founding Gestures of the "New Materialism." *European Journal of Women's Studies* 15 (1), 23–39.

Ahmed, S. (2021). Gender Critical = Gender Conservative. *Feministkilljoys blog*. Posted on October 31, 2021. https://feministkilljoys.com/2021/10/31/gender-critical-gender-conservative/.

Ainsworth, C. (2015). Sex Redefined. *Nature* 518, 288–291. https://doi.org/10.1038/518288a.

Alaimo, S. and Hekman, S. eds. (2008). *Material Feminisms*, Bloomington: Indiana University Press.

Ankermist, F. (2005). *Sublime Historical Experience*, Stanford: Stanford University Press.

Ankersmit, F. and Kellner, H., eds. (1995). *A New Philosophy of History*, Chicago: Chicago University Press.

Arruza, C., Bhattacharya, T., and Fraser, N. (2019). *Feminism for the 99%: A Manifesto*, London, New York: Verso.

Barad, K. (2003). Posthumanist Performativity: Toward an Understanding of How Matter Comes to Matter. *Signs: Journal of Women in Culture and Society* 28 (3), 801–831.

Barclay, K. (2017). New Materialism and the New History of Emotions. *Emotions: History, Culture, Society* 1(1), 161–183.

de Beauvoir, S. (1952). *The Second Sex*, New York: Knopf.

Berger, S. (2022). *History and Identity*, Bloomsbury: London.

Braidotti, R. (2013). *The Posthuman*, Polity: Cambridge.

Braidotti, R. (2018). Posthuman Critical Theory. In Braidotti, R. and Hlavajova, M., eds., *Posthuman Glossary*, London: Bloomsbury, pp. 339–342.

Bravmann, S. (1997). *Queer Fictions of the Past: History, Culture, and Difference*, Cambridge: Cambridge University Press.

Butler, J. (1990). *Gender Trouble, Feminism and the Subversion of Identity*, New York: Routledge.

Butler, J. (1993). *Bodies that Matter: On the Discursive Limits of "Sex,"* New York: Routledge.

Butler, J. (1997). *The Psychic Life of Power: Theories in Subjection*, Stanford: Stanford University Press.

Butler, J. (2004). *Undoing Gender*, New York: Routledge.

Butler, J. (2015). *Notes toward a Performative Theory of Assembly*, Cambridge, MA: Harvard University Press.

Butler, J. (2019). The Backlash against "Gender Ideology" must stop. *The New Statesman*, January 21. www.newstatesman.com/2019/01/judith-butler-backlash-against-gender-ideology-must-stop.

Butler, J. (2024). *Who Is Afraid of Gender?* New York: Farrar, Strauss and Giroux.

Butler, J. and Scott, J. W., eds., (1992). *Feminists Theorize the Political*, New York: Routledge.

Collins, P. H. (2019). *Intersectionality as Critical Social Theory*, Durham and London: Duke University Press.

Córdoba, D., Sáez, J., and Vidarte P., eds. (2005). *Teoría queer: Políticas bolleras, maricas, trans mestizas*, Barcelona: Editorial Egales.

Crenshaw, K. (1991). Mapping the Margins: Intersectionality, Identity Politics, and Violence against Women of Color. *Stanford Law Review* 43 (6), 1241–1299.

Domańska, E. (2019). Posthumanist History. In Tamm, M. and Burke, P., eds., *Debating New Approaches to History*. London: Bloomsbury, 327–352.

Domańska, E. (2021). The Paradigm Shift in the Contemporary Humanities and Social Sciences. In Kuukkanen, J.-M., ed., *Philosophy of History: Twenty-First-Century Perspectives*, London: Bloomsbury, pp. 180–197.

Downs, Laura L. (2019) Gender History. In Tamm, M. and Burke, P., eds., *Debating New Approaches to History*. London: Bloomsbury, 101–115.

Fausto-Sterling, A. (2000). *Sexing the Body: Gender Politics and the Construction of Sexuality*, Basic Books: New York.

Foucault, M. (1980). *The History of Sexuality, Vol. I: An Introduction*, trans. Robert Hurley, New York: Vintage.

Foucault, M. (1984). Nietzsche, Genealogy, History. In Rabinow, P., ed., *The Foucault Reader*, New York: Pantheon Books, pp. 76–100.

Fudge, E. (2019). The Flourishing and Challenging Field of Animal-Human History. *Society & Animals* 27: 647–652.

Gago, V. (2020). *Feminist International: How to Change Everything*, trans. Liz Mason-Deese, New York: Verso.

Germon, J. (2009). *Gender: A Genealogy of an Idea*, London: Palgrave Macmillian.

Halberstam, J. (1998). *Female Masculinity*, Durham: Duke University Press.

Haraway, D. (1988). Situated Knowledges: The Science Question in Feminism and the Privilege of Partial Perspective. *Feminist Studies* 14 (3), 575–599.

Haraway, D. (1991). *Simians, Cyborgs and Women: The Reinvention of Nature*, New York: Routledge.

Harding, S. (1986). *The Science Question in Feminism*, Ithaca: Cornell University Press.

Harding, S., ed. (2004). *The Feminist Standpoint Theory Reader: Intellectual and Political Controversies*, New York: Routledge.

hooks, bell (1984). *Feminist Theory from Margin to Center*, Boston: South End Press.

Kleinberg, E. (2017). *Haunting History: For a Deconstructive Approach to the Past*, Stanford: Stanford University Press.

La Greca, M. I. (2014). The Future of Philosophy of History from Its Narrativist Past: Figuration, Middle Voice Writing and Performativity. *Journal of the Philosophy of History* 8 (2): 196–216.

La Greca, M. I. (2016). Hayden White and Joan W. Scott's Feminist History: The Practical Past, the Political Present and an Open Future. *Rethinking History* 20 (3): 395–413.

La Greca, M. I. (2023). The Other Side of the Linguistic Turn: Theory of History and the Negotiation of Humanity. *Rethinking History* 27 (1), 3–25.

La Greca, M. I. (2024). With or against Hayden White: Reflections on Theory of History and Subject Formation. *History and Theory* 63 (1), 25–44.

La Greca, M. I. and Solana, M. (2024). *El discurso no es destino: debates feministas sobre el cuerpo, la naturaleza y las ciencias*, Buenos Aires: Madreselva.

de Lauretis, T. (1991). Queer Theory: Lesbian and Gay Sexualities: An Introduction. *differences* 3 (2): iii–xviii.

Lugones, M. (2008). The Coloniality of Gender. *World & Knowledges Otherwise* 2 https://globalstudies.trinity.duke.edu/sites/globalstudies.trinity.duke.edu/files/fileattachments/.

Lugones, M. (2010). Toward a Decolonial Feminism. *Hypatia* 25 (4): 742–759.

Majumdar, R. (2022). Postcolonial Theory. In Van Den Akker, C., ed., *The Routledge Companion to Historical Theory*, London and New York: Routledge, pp. 163–178.

Medina, J. (2013). *Epistemology of Resistance: Gender, Racial Oppression, Epistemic Injustice, and Resistant Imaginations*, New York: Oxford University Press.

Meyerowitz, J. (2008). A History of "Gender." *American Historical Review* 113 (5): 1346–1356.

Moulton, M. (2023). "Both Your Sexes": A Non-Binary Approach to Gender History, Trans Studies and the Making of the Self in Modern Britain. *History Workshop Journal* 95, 75–100.

Mudrovcic, M. I. (2024). *Conceptualizing the History of the Present Time*. Cambridge: Cambridge University Press.

Ohara, J. (2022). *The Theory and Philosophy of History, Global Variations*, Cambridge: Cambridge University Press.

Partner, N. (2009). Narrative Persistence: The Post-Postmodern Life of Narrative Theory. In Ankersmit, F., Domańska, E., and Kellner, H., eds., *Refiguring Hayden White*, Stanford: Stanford University Press, pp. 81–104.

Pihlainen, K. (2017). *The Work of History: Constructivism and a Politics of the Past*, New York: Routledge.

Preciado, P. B. (2018). *Countersexual Manifesto*, trans. Kevin Gerry Dunn, New York: Columbia University Press.

Riley, C. (2025). The Archival Is Personal Is Political: Historiography, the Archive, and Feminist Research Methods. In Cooke, J. and Nyhagen, L., eds., *Intersectional Feminist Research Methodologies: Applications in the Social Sciences and Humanities*. London and New York: Routledge, pp. 145–159.

Rubin, G. (1975). The Traffic in Women: Notes on the "Political Economy of Sex." In Reiter, R., ed., *Toward and Anthropology of Women*, Nueva York: Montly Review Press, pp. 157–210.

Rubin, G. (1984). Thinking Sex: Notes for a Radical Theory of the Politics of Sexuality. In Vance, C. S., ed., *Pleasure and Danger: Exploring Female Sexuality*, Boston: Routledge and Kegan Paul, pp. 267–319.

Rubin, G. (2011). *Deviations: A Gayle Rubin Reader*, Durham: Duke University Press.

Runia, E. (2006). Presence. *History and Theory* 45 (1): 1–29.

Salomon, G. (2010). *Assuming a Body: Transgender and Rhetorics of Materiality*. New York: Columbia University Press.

Scott, J. W. (1991). The Evidence of Experience. *Critical Inquiry* 17 (4): 773–797.

Scott, J. W. (1999). *Gender and the Politics of History*. Revised Edition, New York: Columbia University Press.

Scott, J. W. (2011). *The Fantasy of Feminist History*, Durham: Duke University.

Sedgwick, E. F. (1990). *Epistemology of the Closet*, Berkeley: University of California Press.

Serano, J. (2007). *Whipping Girl: A Transsexual Woman on Sexism and the Scapegoating of Femininity*, Berkeley: Seal Press.

Simon, Z. B., Tamm, M., and Domańska, E. (2021). Anthropocenic Historical Knowledge: Promises and Pitfalls. *Rethinking History*, 25(4), 406–439.

Smith, B. G. (1992). Historiography, Objectivity, and the Case of the Abusive Widow. *History and Theory* 31 (4) Beiheft 31: History and Feminist Theory, 15–32.

Smith, B. G. (1995). Gender and the Practices of Scientific History: The Seminar and Archival Research in the Nineteenth Century. *American Historical Review* 100 (4), 1150–1176.

Smith B. G. (2013). *Women's Studies: The Basics*, London and New York: Routledge.

Solana, M. (2024). Átomos queer y bacterias feministas. In La Greca, M. I. and Solana, M., eds., *El discurso no es destino: debates feministas sobre el cuerpo, la naturaleza y las ciencias*, Buenos Aires: Madreselva, pp. 205–225.

Stryker, S. (2006). (De)Subjugated Knowledges: An Introduction to Transgender Studies. In Stryker, S. and Whittle, S., ed., *The Transgender Studies Reader*. New York and London: Routledge, pp. 1–17.

Stryker, S. (2008). *Transgender History*, Berkeley: Seal Press.

Thorpe, H., Brice, J., and Clark, M. (2021). Towards New Materialist Sport History. In Phillips, M. G., Booth, D., and Adams, C., eds., *Routledge Handbook of Sport History*. London: Routledge, pp. 243–250.

Tozzi Thompson, V. (2022). Narrativism. In Van Den Akker, C., ed., *The Routledge Companion to Historical Theory*, London and New York: Routledge, pp. 113–128.

Turner, W. B. (2004). Queer Theory and Queer Studies. In Marc Stein, ed., *Encyclopedia of Lesbian, Gay, Bisexual, and Transgender History in America,* Vol. 2 *H.D. to Queer Theory*, New York: Charles Scribner's Sons, pp. 481–487.

Ware, V. (1992). Moments of Danger: Race, Gender, and Memories of Empire. *History and Theory* 31 (4), 116–137.

Weeks, J. (2016). *What Is Sexual History?* Cambridge: Polity Press.

White, H. (1973). *Metahistory: The Historical Imagination in Nineteenth-Century Europe*, Baltimore: Johns Hopkins University Press.

White, H. (1987). *The Content of the Form: Narrative Discourse and Historical Representation*, Baltimore: Johns Hopkins University Press.

Whittle, S. (2006). Foreword. In Stryker, S. and Whittle, S., ed., *The Transgender Studies Reader*, New York and London: Routledge, pp. xi–xvi.

Wittig, M. (1992). *The Straight Mind and Other Essays*, Boston: Beacon Press.

Historical Theory and Practice

Daniel Woolf
Queen's University, Ontario

Daniel Woolf is Professor of History at Queen's University, where he served for ten years as Principal and Vice-Chancellor, and has held academic appointments at a number of Canadian universities. He is the author or editor of several books and articles on the history of historical thought and writing, and on early modern British intellectual history, including most recently *A Concise History of History* (CUP 2019). He is a Fellow of the Royal Historical Society, the Royal Society of Canada, and the Society of Antiquaries of London. He is married with three adult children.

Editorial Board
Dipesh Chakrabarty, *University of Chicago*
Marnie Hughes-Warrington, *University of South Australia*
Ludmilla Jordanova, *University of Durham*
Angela McCarthy, *University of Otago*
María Inés Mudrovcic, *Universidad Nacional de Comahue*
Herman Paul, *Leiden University*
Stefan Tanaka, *University of California, San Diego*
Richard Ashby Wilson, *University of Connecticut*

About the Series
Cambridge Elements in Historical Theory and Practice is a series intended for a wide range of students, scholars, and others whose interests involve engagement with the past. Topics include the theoretical, ethical, and philosophical issues involved in doing history, the interconnections between history and other disciplines and questions of method, and the application of historical knowledge to contemporary global and social issues such as climate change, reconciliation and justice, heritage, and identity politics.

Cambridge Elements

Historical Theory and Practice

Elements in the Series

Plural Pasts: Historiography between Events and Structures
Arthur Alfaix Assis

The History of Knowledge
Johan Östling and David Larsson Heidenblad

Conceptualizing the History of the Present Time
María Inés Mudrovcic

Writing the History of the African Diaspora
Toyin Falola

Dealing with Dark Pasts: A European History of Auto-Critical Memory in Global Perspective
Itay Lotem

A Human Rights View of the Past
Antoon De Baets

Historians' Autobiographies as Historiographical Inquiry: A Global Perspective
Jaume Aurell

Historiographic Reasoning
Aviezer Tucker

Pragmatism and Historical Representation
Serge Grigoriev

History and Hermeneutics
Paul Fairfield

Testimony and Historical Knowledge: Authority, Evidence and Ethics in Historiography
Jonas Ahlskog

Gender, Theory, and History: On the Knowledge and Politics of Bodies
María Inés La Greca

A full series listing is available at: www.cambridge.org/EHTP

For EU product safety concerns, contact us at Calle de José Abascal, 56–1°,
28003 Madrid, Spain or eugpsr@cambridge.org.

www.ingramcontent.com/pod-product-compliance
Lightning Source LLC
LaVergne TN
LVHW011856060526
838200LV00054B/4357